Danny!
May this book
help you in your!
Journey to Him!
Ronnie...
Phil. 4:13

"I settled into my easy chair intending to read just the first chapter of *The Meaning of a Man*. I didn't get up until I finished the entire book. Ronnie's discussion of spiritual rattlesnakes in chapter 10 ought to be read by every Christian man in America."

STEVE FARRAR, MEN'S LEADERSHIP MINISTRIES AND AUTHOR OF POINT MAN

"This is a book I wish I had read thirty years ago. Dr. Floyd has addressed a long-felt void in the inner being of successful men—how can I be all God meant me to be? *The Meaning of a Man* gives clear direction in achieving the goals your Creator designed for you."

J.B. HUNT, FOUNDER, J.B. HUNT TRANSPORT, INC.

"During the 1995 football season Pastor Floyd took our coaching staff through a weekly Bible study that focused on the concerns of this book. That experience provided valuable insight for us as coaches, husbands, fathers, and members of our community. This is a championship book."

DANNY FORD, HEAD FOOTBALL COACH, UNIVERSITY OF ARKANSAS

"*The Meaning of a Man* was born out of Dr. Ronnie Floyd's profound, soul-stirring experience with the living God. His inspired message calls the men of our age to be champions. No matter who you are or what your background, God wants you to be a winner in Christ and for Christ. This book will show you how. It will change your life."

DR. BILL BRIGHT, FOUNDER AND PRESIDENT, CAMPUS CRUSADE FOR CHRIST INTERNATIONAL

"For the better part of two decades, the male gender has been characterized as a loser. Ronnie Floyd will show you how to be a true spiritual winner."

DENNIS RAINEY, EXECUTIVE DIRECTOR, FAMILYLIFE

"This is a hard-hitting, life-changing book for the man who desires to think and then act as a spiritual champion. I pray thousands of men will read it and heed it."

JACK GRAHAM, SENIOR PASTOR, PRESTONWOOD BAPTIST CHURCH, DALLAS, TEXAS

"Ronnie Floyd has written a captivating book that unlocks the biblical secrets of being a genuine spiritual leader. It is clear, concise, and convicting. There are very few books that I want every man in our church to read—but this is one of them."

RICK WARREN, SADDLEBACK VALLEY COMMUNITY CHURCH, MISSION VIEJO, CALIFORNIA

"I have read many books which have attempted to profile a true spiritual hero—but in this work, Ronnie Floyd nails it. Some books challenge a reader; this one will change a reader!"

ARKANSAS LIEUTENANT GOVERNOR MIKE HUCKABEE

"Don't fail to read and ponder chapter 11 of Dr. Ronnie Floyd's superb book, *The Meaning of a Man*. In fact, read it all. The book is biblically solid, rivetingly interesting, and profoundly written. But chapter 11, "The Courage of a Spiritual Champion," is worth the price of the book. Don't miss it!"

PAIGE PATTERSON, PRESIDENT, SOUTHEASTERN BAPTIST THEOLOGICAL SEMINARY

"Sometimes we need a not-so-subtle reminder to help us focus our attention on things that are really important. This book did that for me. The book focuses specifically on men—their spiritual walk and life's priorities. I found the book to be thought-provoking, challenging and tremendously motivating."

LELAND E. TOLLETT, CHAIRMAN & CHIEF EXECUTIVE OFFICER, TYSON FOODS, INC.

"We are living in a day when a growing number of men want to be all they were meant to be. They have realized that they can reach such a goal only through a growing relationship with God and their family. Women today will benefit from this book because it will help their men become the spiritual leaders of their families—every Christian woman's desire."

DR. TIM LAHAYE, PRESIDENT, FAMILY LIFE SEMINARS, WASHINGTON, D.C.

"Dr. Floyd hits the nail on the head as he challenges men to be spiritual champions in every realm of life. If America is to experience spiritual revival, it will take men who are willing to live out the qualities of a spiritual champion described in this book."

U.S. REPRESENTATIVE TIM HUTCHINSON, 3RD DISTRICT, ARKANSAS

"*The Meaning of a Man* is a critical book for a crucial time. Ronnie Floyd lays out a clear, concise, and very readable book to help men discover what God has designed them to do."

ROBERT MCGEE, FOUNDER, RAPHA TREATMENT CENTERS

"Most books come from the head; *The Meaning of a Man* comes passionately from Ronnie Floyd's heart. If you truly want to be a champion, this book succinctly tells you how. Read it and watch God transform your life through it."

JERRY JOHNSTON, JERRY JOHNSTON FAMILY CRUSADES & RALLIES, OVERLAND PARK, KANSAS

"Chapter after chapter, I was filled with encouragement, hope, and the desire not only to be a winner in my life, but to be a spiritual champion. *The Meaning of a Man* makes me realize that if a revival comes to this country, it must first begin in my heart."

ANDY WILSON, REGIONAL VICE PRESIDENT, WAL-MART STORES, INC.

"Ronnie Floyd is a spiritual coach for spiritual champions. Wives will read this book to discover the definition of a real man. Daughters need to read this book before saying, 'I do.' *The Meaning of a Man* is right on time for fathers and sons."

OREN PARIS, PRESIDENT, INTERNATIONAL MISSIONS NETWORK CENTER, YWAM

"To use a well-worn but very appropriate phrase, 'You have hit the nail on the head!' If a man really has the desire to be all that he can be—in his personal life, in his family life, in the business world and in his spiritual life—he needs to read this book."

W. GREGORY HORTON, FOUNDING PARTNER, RYAN'S FAMILY STEAK HOUSE

"*The Meaning of a Man* explains the clear facts about what a man should do to be a man."

JOE FERGUSON, FORMER NFL QUARTERBACK, BUFFALO BILLS

"This book outlines what every man's ultimate goal should be: to become a spiritual champion. The future of America will be determined by this crucial decision. Don't go into the battle without having read this timely book."

KIRK THOMPSON, PRESIDENT AND CHIEF EXECUTIVE OFFICER, J.B. HUNT TRANSPORT, INC.

"Each page of *The Meaning of a Man* reflects Ronnie Floyd's passion to excel. The book is understandable, convincing, and exceedingly practical."

DR. GEORGE SWEETING, CHANCELLOR, MOODY BIBLE INSTITUTE

"Ronnie Floyd is a man's man who writes with the courage of a champion himself. Anyone who knows the ministry of the great First Baptist Church of Springdale, Arkansas, knows that this church is developing spiritual champions. My prayer is that this book will have wide distribution and will change radically and dramatically the hearts of men."

DR. ADRIAN ROGERS, PASTOR, BELLEVUE BAPTIST CHURCH, CORDOVA, TENNESSEE

THE MEANING OF A
MAN

THE MEANING OF A
MAN

Discovering Your Destiny as a Spiritual Champion

RONNIE W. FLOYD

FOREWORD BY *John Maxwell*

BROADMAN
&HOLMAN
PUBLISHERS

Nashville, Tennessee

© Copyright 1996 • Ronnie W. Floyd
All rights reserved
4261–95
Published by Broadman & Holman Publishers, Nashville, Tennessee

ISBN 0-8054-6195-7
Dewey Decimal Classification: 248.842
Subject Heading: MEN—RELIGIOUS LIFE \ SPIRITUAL LIFE

Library of Congress Cataloging-in-Publication Data
Floyd, Ronnie W., 1955–
    The meaning of a man : discovering your destiny as a spiritual champi-
on \ Ronnie Floyd.
          p.   cm.
   ISBN 0-8054-6195-7
    1. Men—Religious life.   2. Men (Christian theology)   I. Title.
BV4528.2.F57 1996
248.8'42—dc20

Unless otherwise indicated, all Scripture references are from the New American Standard Bible, The Lockman Foundation © 1960, 1962, 1963, 1968,
1971, 1972, 1973, 1975, 1977. Used by permission.

Scripture references marked NIV are from the Holy Bible: New International
Version, © 1973, 1978, 1984 by International Bible Society. Used by permis-
sion of Zondervan Publishing House. All rights reserved. The "NIV" and
"New International Version" trademarks are registered in the United States
Patent and Trademark Office by International Bible Society. Use of either
trademark requires the permission of International Bible Society.

96 97 98 99 00 10 9 8 7 6 5 4 3 2 1

DEDICATION

I dedicate this book to my Dad and Mom, John and Elva Floyd, because they loved me enough to begin shaping my life to become a spiritual champion. Thanks! I love you and will pass on the heritage for generations to come.

CONTENTS

F O R E W O R D

Ronnie Floyd got a wake up call from God on March 28, 1995. On that day, God directed Ronnie to go down a path for forty days that has transformed his life. In fact, it has been the strongest calling of his life since God called him to preach at the age of sixteen. It awakened in him the desire to make a difference . . . the desire to be the man that God intends for him to be. Ronnie calls this being a "spiritual champion." He believes that most men want to be spiritual champions—they want their lives to count, to make a difference. They're not sure how to do it.

This book offers a clear profile of who a spiritual champion is, practical guidelines for becoming a spiritual champion, and pitfalls to watch for in your journey toward signficance. For most of us, this book will not be easy to read. Why? You will be forced to examine every area of your life, your motives, and your priorities. Why you do what you do. The principles that Ronnies uses are sound and biblical. There are no shortcuts on this journey. Each one of us must personally take a stand and answer the call to be a spiritual champion. But the rewards are great!

In more than twenty years of ministry, I have been privileged to know some great spiritual champions. My friend Ronnie is unequaled in his passion and his desire to make a difference, to make his life count . . . to be a spiritual champion. Personally, I can think of no greater legacy as a man than to make a difference in my lifetime for my children and my children's children. That's what this book is all about. I challenge you to answer this call. Enjoy your journey.

Dr. John C. Maxwell
Founder, INJOY

ACKNOWLEDGMENTS

May each reader of this book know that my heart overflows with gratitude to God for what He has done in my life which has served as the spark for writing this book. God and God alone deserves the praise.

Many times the tools that God uses in our lives are people. The Lord used Barbara Freeman, my former administrative assistant, to help generate the manuscript into book form. My editor Steve Halliday, held the standard high and did a superb job of guiding me through this project. Two young preachers, Rex Griffin and Jay Lowder, assisted me in the research for this book. Craig Miller, one of my associates who is now a full-time evangelist, dreamed with me through this project on a flight from Denver.

I am very thankful to Bucky Rosenbaum, Kirk Freeman, Chuck Wilson, and all the friends at Broadman & Holman Publishers for placing this book in your hands.

I am incredibly grateful to God for my wife, Jeana, and our two boys, Josh and Nick, who pay the price with me in my zeal and preoccupation in getting ideas from my heart to the printed page. I love each of you and appreciate your patience and understanding.

I thank each of you for desiring to grow in your understanding of your meaning of a man.

When God Comes

May I tell you something? I want to be a spiritual champion, and I think you want to be one, too. Just imagine what a nation and a world this would be if men everywhere decided it was time to become the spiritual champions God means for them to be.

My own wake up call to this possibility came early on the morning of March 28, 1995, while reading God's Word in my private devotions. In a few short but precious moments, God spoke to me in a profound way. It could very well be the clearest call I have received since I was sixteen years old and God called me to preach the gospel of Jesus Christ.

God called me to fast and pray for forty days, focusing on spiritual revival in America, in my church, and in my life. God wanted me to seek Him with every fiber of my being, with all my heart and soul.

My forty-day journey with God began on the evening of April 15 and the fast wasn't broken until the evening of May 25. Those forty days with God changed my life. I have no desire to return to the old me that existed before April 15.

In those forty days with God I experienced spiritual revival. God manifested His presence to me—and not all of that is easy or pleasant. I had to face some things about myself that I did not like. I was urged to deal with and overcome sins that had damaged my life for years. While I was not involved in "pagan-type" sins, sin is sin. It had invaded and encamped in the secret chambers of my heart and was robbing me of consistent spiritual joy, power, and victory.

Yet by the end of the fast, fears and bondage turned into spiritual power and freedom. In those forty marvelous days, God transformed my life.

When it was all over, the Lord permitted me to tell my church about what had occurred during my forty-day journey with God. It was Sunday, June 4, 1995, a date etched into the memories of everyone present that day at First Baptist Church in Springdale, Arkansas.

I was open and honest about my failings and I straightforwardly declared the message that I believed God wanted my congregation to hear. I described my heartfelt belief that God is going to bring a great spiritual revival to America that will transcend all denominational lines, cultural distinctives, ethnic groups, and races. I said that I believed a remnant of God's people in America will experience the manifested presence of God in which countless thousands of souls will come to know Jesus Christ as Savior and Lord.

Fifteen minutes into my message, I knew something unusual was up. The schedule restraints, the live radio broadcast, the national television broadcast—none of it mattered. The service lasted over two and a half hours, well past the sanctified hour of high noon. Yet that evening, 70 percent of the morning crowd returned for a service that lasted more than four hours. We didn't leave until after 10:00 P.M.

On this day, time did not matter. An hour seemed like ten minutes. People perched on the edges of their seats one minute and threw themselves on their faces before God the next. Very few wanted to go home even after the lengthy services concluded. Why?

> **On this day, time did not matter. An hour seemed like ten minutes. Very few wanted to go home. Why? God came.**

God came.

Grown men sobbed openly, flat on their faces before God, their hot tears flowing like life-giving rivers. It was a display of brokenness beyond anything I had ever witnessed.

You might expect such mourning over the loss of a loved one. But this time, the mourning was over sin. Real men mourned deeply over their sin.

No one cared what others might think of them; the time for brutal honesty before God had come. The time for games had passed. No one wanted to play "hide and seek" with God. Men shed their masks for a genuine encounter with the Holy One of Israel.

Mighty conviction swept the room. Hundreds of people flooded the altar in repentance even before a public invitation was extended. With intense desperation men strove to get things right with God, whatever the cost. Men faced their sin, confessed it, repented of it, and were delivered from it. Sins of lust, alcohol, drugs, stealing from God, and dishonesty were all enthusiastically abandoned. Relationships were made right as men led their families to the altar—the first time some of these fathers had ever prayed with their wives and children. Spiritual leaders were being born before my eyes and I knew our church would never be the same again. Yes, this day was different! Why?

God came.

God is holy, and when He descended upon His people on this day, He came the way He always is: Holy. Many in the congregation could only remain silent, for never before had they sensed the power and reality of God's infinite holiness. Today it could not be missed.

The holiness of God exposed sin, burning away its dark cloak and revealing it for the cancer it is. On this day, sin seemed so wrong, so personal, so offensive toward God. It could be tolerated no longer. Although the congregation before me included the same people with the same problems and the same sin that had sat there week after week, in a moment everything had changed. What was different? Why had everything so radically transformed?

God came.

Whenever God comes, things change. No one is ever the same once they have encountered the manifested presence of God. I know I never will be.

Even now it is not easy for me to write about this experience. Chills race up and down my spine as I write. Adjectives and personal testimonies fail to capture the essence of what happened that day. How can mere language describe the life-changing force that descends on a people when God visits them in His infinite power and holiness? *God came!*

> " Whenever God comes, things change. No one is ever the same once they have encountered the manifested presence of God. "

I know the modern world is skeptical of such terminology, but it can say what it wants. Those of us who were there know its overwhelming reality. Preschoolers, children, teenagers, college students, baby busters, baby boomers, and all the rest will always remember how God came on this day and changed all of us forever.

It was the greatest move of God I have ever had the privilege of experiencing—yet I believe it is only the beginning of what God wants to do among us. I am convinced God wants to duplicate it throughout America and the world.

We saw spiritual champions born that day, champions that God will use to change our little corner of the world. But God does not want this to stop with Springdale, Arkansas. He doesn't want it to stop with the United States or North America or the Western Hemisphere. He's looking for spiritual champions all over the globe. And He wants to start with *you*.

God wants to use you as a spiritual champion to make a difference in this world. He is calling you to become all that He created you to be. And He wants to start today.

It is past time for men to get real. It is time to stop playing games, especially in our spiritual lives. Too many things hang in the balance:

- Physical treasures such as our jobs, careers, and finances.
- Spiritual treasures such as moral purity, integrity, and a clear conscience.
- Human treasures such as our wives, children, and grandchildren.
- Eternal treasures such as joy, peace, and purpose.

All of these hang in the balance, as does our entire future. All are determined by the quality of our spiritual lives. And that is determined by our own choices.

I will always be grateful for what God did in my heart and in my congregation in 1995. But I can never forget that first the Lord had to do some things in *me* before He was free to do some things in our *church*. He had to do some things in *me* before He could do some things in my *family*. It began with me—just as it must begin with you.

> **God wants to use you as a spiritual champion to make a difference in this world. And He wants to start today.**

This book is not about fasting and prayer, even though you will see a few such references scattered throughout the manuscript. It is not a book about spiritual revival, even though you may be encouraged toward this great need in our day.

This book is about men being spiritual champions. It is about coming to understand who you are in Christ and about how you can make certain that your life will make a difference. It is about leaving a permanent mark on the lives of others. It is about being a "difference-maker." Spiritual champions cannot help but make a difference.

If you want to play games with God, this book is not for you. If you shy away from coming clean with God and others, then lay this book aside. This book is not called *Religious Games 101*. If you have no desire to leave a major, positive mark on this earth, then you have the wrong book in your hand.

But if you want to become all that God created you to be—if you're willing to be stretched beyond your present comfort zone—then you've come to the right place. *The Meaning of a Man* is the book for you.

I believe men all across this spiritually dry land are looking for something and someone authentic. I believe men want to be "difference-makers." I believe they want to find a way to stop believing the junk Satan places into their minds, to stop accepting the hellish lie that they cannot be something great for God. They're tired of departmentalizing their lives. They want wholeness. They want authenticity. They want to make a difference. They want to be spiritual champions.

But that all hangs on a choice. Face it: As your spiritual life goes, so goes the rest of your life.

You *can* make a difference. Why not step up to the winner's circle and receive your rightful spiritual blessings? When you make that step toward God, He will place His indelible mark on your life. Then, in Christ, you will begin to exude spiritual confidence that you have never before enjoyed.

In fact, I'll let you in on a secret: You will begin to live like the spiritual champion *God has already enabled you to become*.

PART ONE

How to Want It

C H A P T E R   O N E

You Can Make a Difference

*T*ime magazine called it, "A Blow to the Heart." At 9:02 A.M. on April 19, 1995, a thunderous explosion tore apart the Alfred P. Murrah Federal Building in Oklahoma City. One moment people were enjoying the calm of a pleasant Wednesday morning; the next instant hundreds of innocent victims were blown to bits in a senseless act of terrorism. Within minutes of the blast, news cameras brought the carnage directly into the living rooms of a horrified nation.

We all watched with tear-stained eyes as paramedics, doctors, firefighters, policemen, off-duty public servants, and uninjured passers-by raced to the scene, risking their lives to save strangers. Words cannot adequately describe the courageous actions of these instant heroes. Yet the work took its toll. One reporter said,

> The rescuers wept as they cradled them, limp and weightless; fire fighters could not bear to look down at the children in their arms. "Find out who did this," one told Oklahoma Governor Frank Keating. "All that I have found are a baby's finger and an American flag."[1]

A single poignant image quickly came to symbolize this American tragedy. A stricken Chris Fields, clad in his smudged fire fighting gear, is shown cradling one-year-old Baylee Almon, her limp body covered with blood from an apparent gash to the head.

Yes, it was a blow to the heart. A blow not only to the heartland of America, but to the heart of every American as well.

While Chris Fields became the best-known rescuer that day, he was far from the only hero. In that frightful moment of crisis, heroes materialized from everywhere. Selflessness replaced selfishness. Passion replaced passivity. Intentionality replaced indifference. Rescuers acted against the norm and beyond the expected. They determined to risk everything they were and had for the sake of others, acting even without knowing whether anyone was left alive under the rubble. That is heroism. That is courage. That is making a difference.

The American people owe a great debt to those selfless, passionate, and determined rescue workers in the Oklahoma City bombing. These were "Difference-Makers" with a capital D.

This One Thing

There is one thing I must know concerning any activity I do in life. I must always know I am making a difference. Frustration results whenever I am unsure whether I am making a difference. It does not matter if it concerns my walk with Christ, my church, my relationships, coaching my boys' football teams, or sitting in a meeting—I need to know I am making a difference. If I am not, I grow frustrated. If I am, then I am fulfilled.

I'm sure I am not unique in this. I am convinced all men want to know they are making a difference. Some men work ten to fifteen hours a day to make a difference, but go home frustrated. They just don't feel they're accomplishing anything. Other men pursue fulfillment through community service. They tolerate their daily routines in order to make a difference in other arenas of life. Still others move from one project to another, seeking to meet this deep need.

It's simply a fact of life that most men I know want to make a difference. They want their lives to count. They want to leave their mark behind. They want to leave the world a better place than it was when they arrived on the scene.

Their only problem? They're puzzled about how to do it.

What Every Man Wants

For at least twenty years, I have walked closely with men from all walks of life. I have been a friend to many of these men and a pastor to many others. I have observed them all and have learned much from them. I discovered that they all share some common desires about what they want out of life. So what do men want?

1. *Worth.* Men have a significant need to feel that they have worth. This need is amplified by the role we play in our families as provider and leader. Many things contribute to our perception of our own worth, such as the kind of role models we had in our formative years, the guidance and teaching we received in our families regarding our responsibilities as bread winners, and so on. For most men, one enormous aspect of sensing their worth is their ability to make a difference in life. If they feel they are not making much of a difference—if they believe the world wouldn't miss them for an instant should they suddenly disappear—then it's probable they won't feel "worth" very much.

2. *Identity.* A man's sense of identity, like his sense of worth, begins to formulate at an early age. As men, we want our identity to be unique, our own, with our peculiar stamp of individuality. We want to be our own man.

Gary, a typical "Christian type of guy," was eagerly searching for his identity. The only problem was he attempted to discover his identity in all of the wrong things. He sought it in gold, glory, and girls. These three have sunk many men. They also sank Gary.

He lost his wife and her loyal love. He lost his children, their respect and approval. He eventually lost his career. All because he was trying to be someone. Who was that someone? That someone for Gary is the same someone we have all sought periodically. The straw man! We have him pictured in our minds as being the perfect guy, but he does not exist.

3. *A satisfying career.* Most men weave grand dreams during their college years of what they will become after they receive their degrees. They nurture visions of "setting the world on fire," excelling in their fields, and moving upward in record time. At some point, after realizing that not everyone can reach the top, every man must come to terms with what kind of satisfaction work can bring.

In his book, *Halftime,* Bob Buford challenges men to change the game plan for their lives from success to significance. He writes that men pursue success the first half of their lives, but this quest always ends in a need for something more. In a time of evaluation, each man must ask himself the hard questions of life. If a man has answered these questions correctly, he will not get caught up in the "success-syndrome" of our day, but will desire to be and do something significant in the last half of his life.

Are you looking for a new aerobic exercise? Then go outside, determine which way the wind is blowing, and chase after it. You'll quickly discover it's an exercise in futility.

4. *A good relationship with his wife.* Every man wants a meaningful and fulfilling relationship with his wife. He wants to know his wife stands beside him in all things. He desires that she encourage him and respect him. He wants to be loved by her physically, to enjoy the thrill of being truly one with her. He wants to be able to communicate with her about the things that are heaviest on his heart.

I know this is true of me. Let me introduce you to my sweetheart, Jeana. She is the daughter of a pastor, raised on the plains of West Texas. We met in college, fell in love, and married on the last day of 1976. We love being together. We are friends—best friends. We are committed to each other's success.

Jeana is everything I need her to be for me. She walks beside me through everything. She encourages me at all times. She loves me physically the way I like to be loved. She listens to me when I need to bare my heart. We have had many all night conversations; some may have started with misunderstanding, but every one of them has concluded with admiration and love reaffirmed.

Our relationship has its ups and downs like everyone else's, but we both know our mutual commitment to each other stays rock steady. I don't know how I'd make it through life without being able to count on Jeana—my wife, best friend, and lover.

5. *Children who love him.* As the family crowds around the bed of a dying father and husband, time seems to creep along. The smell of death fills the room. Silence and whispers replace noise and laughter. All wait to hear a word from the man of the family. As he makes his last statement, gasping for every breath, his body wracked with pain, he never says, "I just want all of you to know: I wish I had spent more time at the office!"

My kids are everything to me. I plan my schedule so that I can be a part of the things that are important to them. More than once activities and opportunities have been canceled or delayed so I could attend one of their sports activities. These guys are my heroes.

This year Joshua will turn the magic sixteen. Nicholas will finally become what he has acted like for two years, a teenager. In a few short years, all that my kids have been taught will be tested and tried. How I want them to succeed!

As I have ministered across America, I have discovered that men desperately want to be able to communicate with their children. Even if the words are few in those transitional adolescent years, a few words to a dad are worth a million bucks.

Men want their children to respect them. I know I respect my dad. There never has been a time when I have not and there never shall be a time when I will not. He is my dad! He sacrificed much while I was growing up so that I might have more, and he deserves my honor and appreciation.

Every man wants the respect and love of his children. He craves it. He longs for it. And happy is the man who has it.

6. *Community.* Every man lives in community. We relate, we interact, we seek those who share similar circumstances and interests. The common aspect of our lives may be location, a civic club, church, hobbies, or vocation, but we are creatures who seek our own kind. Sometimes the common factor is literally our community, living in close proximity in a neighborhood or town. Men want to have influence in this domain as well. No doubt this is linked to the kind of environment we want for our families, an environment that will enable them to grow and thrive. We want to know that we are impacting the community in which we live.

What's the Difference?

Although the Rolling Stones are a long way from being godly role models, even this hard-living rock group managed to get at least one thing right. One of their most famous songs reminds us, "You can't always get what you want." That's true. Nobody gets everything they want in life—and the infuriating thing is that often it's the things we want the most that are the most difficult to lay our hands on.

Consider the list we just discussed. Every man wants worth and identity. Every man wants a successful career. Every man longs for a meaningful relationship with his wife and family. Every man desires to have a positive impact upon his community. Yet most men fail to achieve these things. Why? How can such important desires elude us? It's because most of us fail to realize that these things simply will not materialize *apart from a miracle.*

You see, the difference is in the difference! The difference you make *with* your life is totally contingent on the difference God makes *in* you. The difference you make in others will never be any greater than the difference which has been made in you by Jesus Christ.

> **The difference you make in others will never be any greater than the difference which has been made in you by Jesus Christ.**

The dent we can make in our world will be insignificant without the power of Jesus Christ flowing through our lives. Without a vital relationship with Jesus, the difference we will be able to make will be no greater than a tiny ripple in the vastness of the ocean. But with Him, it can be like moving a mighty mountain chain. The impression we make will be "God-size" when we allow the power of Jesus Christ to flow through us. God can do more in a moment than you and I can do in a lifetime!

You Plus Jesus Equals a Difference

In the game of life there are winners and there are losers. There are no ties. That's true for all of us. When our lives are over, we will either have won or lost. At that time, it will be too late to do anything about our situations. Today, however, it is not too late to affect the outcome; in fact, it is just the right time.

Let's cut to the real issue. Gentlemen, with Jesus, you will win. Without Jesus, you will lose. That's it. It's that simple. Jesus wants to make you into a difference maker.

Two famous verses show the huge difference it makes whether you are trying to make it through life with or without Jesus. The Master Himself reminded us of our destiny without Him: "I am the vine, you are the branches; he who abides in Me, and I in him, he bears much fruit; for apart from Me you can do nothing" (John 15:5).

On the other hand, consider what God says through Paul in Philippians 4:13: "I can do all things through Him who strengthens me."

God never lies. He wants to make a difference in you—just as He has in countless others—so that you can make a difference in those around you. This is serious business. Life business. Eternal business.

Take Your Place in the Winner's Circle

My dictionary defines a champion as "one who wins first prize or place in a contest; one who is acknowledged to be better than all others." I think the apostle Paul would approve of such a definition; apparently he was quite a fan of sporting events, especially track and field. I guess if you can't be a fan of the Dallas Cowboys, you might as well hook up with the Ancient Spartans!

We know Paul must have been an avid sports fan because so many of his letters use illustrations taken from athletic competition. One of the most famous is found in 1 Corinthians 9:24-27. It's a great text, and I consider it central for the message of this book. Here's what Paul had to say:

> Do you not know that those who run in a race all run, but *only* one receives the prize? Run in such a way that you may win. And everyone who competes in the games exercises self-control in all things. They then *do it* to receive a perishable wreath, but we an imperishable. Therefore I run in such a way, as not without aim; I box in such a way, as not beating the air; but I buffet my body and make it my slave, lest possibly, after I have preached to others, I myself should be disqualified.

This passage is about champions—spiritual champions. They're *spiritual* champions because they understand that the real competition is not merely for a chance at a bronze or silver or gold medal, but to win eternal souls. Their chief aim in life is to make the biggest difference they can, and they know that the best way to do that is by allowing God to work through them to gain spiritual victory. And they're spiritual *champions* because they don't merely enter the race, they run to win. They give everything they have so that one day they can stand in the winner's circle.

This entire book is focused on this critical theme. I want to challenge you and equip you to become a spiritual champion. Too many men are satisfied merely with getting their names written on the team roster; they have no interest in actually running the race. They know they're on the winning side and that one day they'll be riding along in a ticker tape parade held to honor the victors, but they shy away from putting in the hard training it takes to become a champion.

Paul would never be satisfied with such a flabby, couch potato mentality. He knew he was in a race, *and he intended to win*. Neither was he satisfied to run all by himself. Although he knew that only one runner could win the sporting events he was so fond of, he also knew that in the spiritual race, God had arranged for the possibility of multiple winners. That is why the apostle challenges us in verse 24, "run in such away as to get the prize" (NIV).

> **"** That's the challenge for us: *Run in such a way as to get the prize.* **"**

Men, that's the challenge for us: *Run in such a way as to get the prize.* Not everyone will get it. In fact, not everyone on the winning side will even try for it. I confess with great regret that many, perhaps even most, of the Christians I know are content to watch teammates run; they never even put on their Nikes. Of course, none of them are spiritual champions. And they'll never get the prize.

I believe that our culture and even our churches have largely forgotten there is a place today for hard toil, for great deeds, for energetic striving after extraordinary feats. That's what a champion does. He's not willing merely to enter the race; he wants to win it. And how does he win it? By preparing for it. Paul said that everyone who competes in the games goes into strict training. They know that's the only way they'll win. Great desire is only a part of the package needed to win; strict training is the other part.

That's what this book is about. You might think of it as a "Training Manual for Spiritual Champions." I don't claim that you and I can become spiritual champions simply by desiring to stand in the winner's circle. As Paul knew, it takes hard work to get there. But man, is it worth it!

The apostle reminds us that athletes go into strict training not "to get a crown that will not last; but . . . to get a crown that will last forever" (NIV). If only we could realize how high the stakes are! Spiritual champions run in a race in which the fate of countless lives hang in the balance. They train hard not only to win the prize, but because they understand that God has promised to empower their efforts to make an eternal difference in the lives they touch. Yes, the stakes are high—unimaginably high.

We need spiritual champions, and we need *you* to be one of them!

But if you want to be a spiritual champion, if you want to win the prize, you have to do more than just go through the motions. Paul said, "I do not run like a man running aimlessly; I do not fight like a man beating the air. No, I beat my body and make it my slave so that after I have preached to others, I myself will not be disqualified for the prize."

> **If you want to be a spiritual champion, if you want to win the prize, you have to do more than just go through the motions**

Will you accept the challenge? Do you want to be a spiritual champion? The first step is to decide that you will do what it takes to become a spiritual champion. Then you must train to accomplish your goal. Then, and only then, will you be enabled to take your place in the champion's circle.

All of this, of course, depends on building a vital, growing relationship with Jesus Christ. Without a personal relationship with Jesus Christ, none of us can become a spiritual champion. "Without me," Jesus said, "you can do nothing." But wherever Jesus goes, He makes a difference. Whoever He enters, He changes. *You plus Jesus equals a difference.*

Would you like to let Jesus change you? Would you like to let Jesus make a difference in you? You will not find what I am talking about in joining a church. You will not find it in being baptized. You will not find it in living a good and responsible life. You will only discover it when you determine to give first priority to your personal relationship with Jesus,[2] then take the appropriate steps to carry out your determination. That's the only way you'll win the prize. And that's the only way you'll ever become a spiritual champion.

The Mark of a Spiritual Champion

Jesus wants you to be a spiritual champion. And what is the mark of being a spiritual champion? It's that Jesus Christ has made a major difference in your life. You have been changed. Your thought patterns are different. Your decision-making processes are different. Your outlook on life is different. Your relationships are different. Your attitude is different. You are a new person, a determined person—a spiritual champion.

The Ultimate Champion, Jesus Christ, wants to place His mark on you. It's the mark of difference, of change. He's calling you to be a spiritual champion, to make a difference everywhere you go. Jesus can enable you to make a difference in the lives of each person you touch. They will see you as a "difference maker." Remember, you plus Jesus Christ equals a difference! He is not only changing you, but through you He wants to change others. He changes circumstances. He changes situations. He invites you to become His vessel of change. You can make a difference!

The Time Is Now

The alarm clock is going off in our nation today. America finds itself in a grave spiritual crisis. The profound moral, ethical, political, economic, and leadership dilemmas that confront our country have developed because of a deep and growing spiritual vacuum. This is no time to hit the snooze button!

Where are the spiritual champions who will help lead our children back to safety and sanity? Where are the godly heroes, the men of renown, who through faith in God can once again conquer kingdoms, administer justice, and gain what was promised? Whose weakness is turned to strength, and who become powerful in battle and rout foreign armies? (*see* Hebrews 11:33-34).

Where are they? I'll tell you. *You're reading this book!*

> Now is the time for you to realize that you can make a difference. Now is the time for you to *choose* to become a spiritual champion.

Now is the time for you to realize that you can make a difference. Now is the time for you to *choose* to become a spiritual champion. If those rescue workers in Oklahoma City had hesitated one moment in the midst of the tragedy, precious lives would have been lost. Those rescuers believed they could make a difference and their selflessness, passion, and determination proved to the world that they *could* make a difference.

The time is now for you to arise and make a difference. Spiritual champions do not ignore the alarm. They never press the snooze button. Spiritual champions are dedicated to winning the prize, not just for themselves but for their loved ones as well.

Passivity in spiritual matters is one of the major reasons our nation is experiencing such a spiritual crisis. Spiritual champions are as intentional as the heroes in the Oklahoma City bombing. Indifference is unacceptable in a time of spiritual crisis.

I know you want to make a difference. Most men I know go for the gusto in every area of their lives . . . except in their spiritual lives. They simply do not believe they can make the cut in spiritual matters. So instead they spend their energy, time, talents, and vision on things that have no eternal value.

That is why so many men go to their graves unfulfilled.

The dreary label "unfulfilled" does not have to deface your own tombstone. God wants you to be a spiritual champion. He's calling you to make a difference, a significant difference that will not be forgotten the moment your loved ones drive away from the graveside. As a spiritual champion, you can make the kind of difference that will not only outlive you, but your children and grandchildren as well.

You plus Jesus equals a difference. Men, welcome to the champion's circle. It is time to receive all that God has for you!

S T U D Y   Q U E S T I O N S

1. How important is it to you to make a difference with your life? Explain.

2. In what areas of life do you believe you are currently making a difference? In what areas of life do you wish you had a greater influence? What would it take for you to have a greater impact in those areas? Explain.

3. Ronnie lists several items which most men really want. Discuss each one, both describing what each one is and how important it is to you:

A. Worth

B. Identity

C. A satisfying career

D. A good relationship with wife

E. Children who love him

F. Community

4. Ronnie writes, "The difference you make in others will never be any greater than the difference which has been made in you by Jesus Christ." What do you think he means, and do you agree with him? Why or why not?

5. Read John 15:5 and compare it with Philippians 4:13. Separately, what do these two verses teach? What do they teach when taken together? What is your personal connection to these verses?

6. Read 1 Corinthians 9:24-27. What is the "prize" Paul talks about? Who gets it? Who doesn't get it? What does it take to get it? Do you think you'll get it? Explain.

7. How would you describe your current relationship with Christ? Close? Arms-length? Growing? Stagnant? What would you like it to be? What would it take to bring it to that level?

8. What "mark" separates you from the crowd? Or are you indistinguishable from it? Explain.

9. Read Hebrews 11:33,34. What is possible for a man of faith, according to this passage? How does this relate to present-day challenges? How does it relate to the challenges you face?

10. If you went to your grave today, would you go fulfilled, or unfulfilled? Explain.

The Dynasty That Never Ends

I am an avid sports fan and football is my favorite sport. There is nothing like sitting in an emotionally-charged stadium on a cool, fall evening or a blustery winter day, and watching a football game. It doesn't matter if it's kid's day, junior or senior high school, college, or professional—as long it's football, I love it.

Two vivid memories remain with me from my childhood and both involve football. I used to play the game for hours by myself. That's not possible, you say? You're wrong. With a potent imagination, anything's possible.

I'd imagine the whole game. I threw the ball to myself. I ran until I felt it was reasonable to be tackled. I jigged. I jagged. Every game came down to a final play, win or lose. The play always went to me and I always made the winning run, the winning pass, or the winning catch. I was incredible. I even did the play-by-play.

I also have unforgettable memories of Sunday afternoons, hanging out at my friend David McLarry's house after church. We both loved football.

Our agenda was determined by what time the Dallas Cowboys were scheduled to play. Landry, Meredith, Perkins, Lilly, Hayes—those guys played the game not just for money, but because they loved it. If the Cowboys had a late game, we went outside, regardless of weather, and played until they came on. Once our beloved Cowboys took the field, we plunked down in front of the TV and set up our own electric football set.

Remember, this was in the days before video games. Long before Nintendo or Sega Genesis, there was electric football. It took forever to play. You set up your team of eleven plastic men, flipped the switch, and watched them buzz all over the vibrating metal field. Each play might last for a good chunk of a quarter—but what a game! The only time David and I ever fought was when it came time to decide who would be the Cowboys. Since he was older, bigger, and uglier than I, he always got his way.

Oh, man. There was nothing like it! The Dallas Cowboys on television with semi-good reception . . . electric football . . . a good friend. What a childhood! What a life!

You know, I'm still a Dallas Cowboys fan. I have been with them when they were nothing, I suffered with them through many "near championships," I celebrated with them when they won it all. Even during the difficult days of transition between Tom Landry and Jimmy Johnson, I was with them. Tom Landry is one of my heroes and one of these days I hope I get to meet him, but understand: I am a Dallas Cowboys fan. Tom Landry. Jimmy Johnson. Barry Switzer. It just doesn't matter. The blue, the silver, and the star will always be a part of my life.

On at least three occasions I have thought the Dallas Cowboys would be a dynasty forever. I thought they would always be champions. Yet every time talk of a dynasty began to fill the airwaves, unexpected defeat and disappointment silenced the talk.

The *Random House College Dictionary* defines the word "dynasty" as "a sequence of rulers from the same family, stock, or group." It adds that a dynasty is "to rule of such a sequence."

A dynasty occurs when a person, group, family, or team reigns for a long time. They are number one, the champions, for an extended period.

Yet no dynasty lasts forever. It does not matter whether it's the Dallas Cowboys, a thriving corporation, or a royal family; an endless dynasty is impossible. Why is that?

First, all organizations are made up of imperfect human beings with limitations. If an injury sidelines an Emmitt Smith, Michael Irvin, or Troy Aikman at the wrong time, the championship can be lost and the dynasty threatened. Beyond that, all human beings make mistakes. In the National Football Conference championship game in 1995 against the San Francisco Forty-Niners, Cowboy mistakes made it impossible to dig out and win the game.

Second, all organizations change. Players retire or get traded. Coaches leave. Teams change hands. Change is a part of life and it makes a perpetual dynasty impossible.

Third, human dynasties are always done in by human pride. If one player thinks he is worth more money than he is being paid, his ego could destroy championship potential. Pride inevitably destroys unity, and unity is essential to any team or organization. You don't win championships without pulling together as a team.

While a championship may be won here and there, a perpetual dynasty simply will never occur. Dynasties simply do not last forever.

Except for one.

What Is a Real Champion?

Since this is a book about spiritual champions, it's time for all of us to consider more deeply what a champion *is*. What is a real champion?

The dictionary defines a champion as "a person who has defeated all opponents in a competition," "anyone who takes first place in a competition," or "a person who fights for or defends any person or cause." Various synonyms for the word include "winner," "victor," "defender," "protector," and "advocate."

A real champion is pre-eminent in a given field. He takes to the field in order to uphold a given cause. He is a defender, a warrior. A champion is the only one still standing when the battle is over. All of his opponents lie defeated.

The Only Ultimate Spiritual Champion

Only one person in history has defeated all of His opponents. Only one person has taken first place in all competitions. Only one person fights for and defends the cause of all men. Only one person is *the* mighty warrior, *the* winner, and *the* victor.

Who is it?

His name is Jesus Christ. He has a dynasty without end. He has defeated all of His opponents. He is in first place in everything. He had all men in mind when He fought on behalf of their futures.

> **Jesus Christ has a dynasty without end. He has defeated all of His opponents. He is in first place in everything.**

Jesus is the only super champion—the peerless, ultimate spiritual champion.

The most pivotal event in human history is the crucifixion of Jesus Christ. We even measure time in relation to the cross, the place where Jesus Christ became the only ultimate spiritual champion.

If we ever hope to become a spiritual champion, we must understand how Jesus Christ became the only ultimate spiritual champion. Our own status as a spiritual champion is totally wrapped up in Jesus Christ. The moment we surrendered our lives to Jesus as our Lord and Savior, we embraced all that Jesus did for us on the cross. What took place at the cross affected us for eternity. What happened at the cross? How did Jesus Christ become the ultimate spiritual champion?

By Defeating All of His Opponents

At the cross and through the resurrection, Jesus Christ defeated all of His opponents. Colossians 2:13-15 tells us:

And when you were dead in your transgressions and the uncircumcision of your flesh, He made you alive together with Him, having forgiven us all our transgressions, having canceled out the certificate of debt consisting of decrees against us and which was hostile to us; and He has taken it out of the way, having nailed it to the cross. When He had disarmed the rulers and authorities, He made a public display of them, having triumphed over them through Him.

These verses picture the truth about what happened on the cross when Jesus died for you.

The Enemy of Self Was Defeated

The biggest obstacle we face in living as a spiritual champion is self. Colossians 2:13 makes it clear that at one time your spirit was dead in sin. Ephesians 2:1 reaffirms this by saying, "And you were dead in your trespasses and sins."

A person is dead spiritually until Jesus Christ brings him into spiritual life. At the cross, Jesus made your spirit alive together with Him. This became reality when Jesus Christ came into your life.

Self is the agent that brought death to the human spirit. Self served sin and it is sin that brings spiritual death.

When you embraced Jesus Christ, self was crucified. You could not be saved eternally from the power and penalty of your sin until you realized that you could not save yourself. Self died the day you embraced Jesus Christ. Romans 6:6-7 says,

> Knowing this, that our old self was crucified with *Him*, that our body of sin might be done away with, that we should no longer be slaves to sin; for he who has died is freed from sin.

Your old self was crucified, put to death, on the cross with Jesus. Otherwise, there would be no way for you to live like a spiritual champion.

When we are struggling with what seems to be a losing battle with our own flesh, we need help. Fortunately, it's available to each of us in a 2:20. What is that? A remembrance and understanding of Galatians 2:20, which says,

> I have been crucified with Christ; and it is no longer I who live, but Christ lives in me; and the *life* which I now live in the flesh I live by faith in the Son of God, who loved me, and delivered Himself up for me.

You and I have been crucified with Christ. In order to live in the present we have to look back at the cross. At the cross we learn what happened to us; now we live it out. The enemy of self already has been defeated.

None of us can live the Christian life. We cannot live the life of a spiritual champion. We are dead. We have no rights. Each day we must remember that our "old man" is dead; otherwise, the life of Jesus Christ cannot live through us.

> God does not want our best. The best of our best will end in spiritual defeat and continual frustration.

Giving our best, doing our best, being our best is not what the life of a spiritual champion is all about. The life of a spiritual champion is about letting the ultimate spiritual champion, Jesus Christ, live through us. Jesus' death on the cross defeated the enemy of self. But as good as that is, that's not all that happened at the cross.

The Enemy of Sin Was Defeated

At the cross the power of sin was defeated. At the cross, the right of sin to rule over you became inoperative, powerless, and nullified.

Sin was defeated because Jesus Christ canceled the condemnation of God's righteous Law by paying the price for our sin. The Law makes us aware of our need for God and displays publicly that we are sinners who fall short of God's expectations. At the cross, Jesus satisfied all requirements of the Law. We have no obligation to keep it in order to be acceptable; rather, we recognize the character of God that the Law exemplifies. The Law embodies God's holiness, justice, and love. Spiritual champions are no longer under the condemnation of the Law, but are free in the Spirit of Christ and in the grace of God.

Jesus Christ ended all slavery to sin for those who have accepted Him as Lord and Savior. Spiritual champions have been freed from *all* sin. There is no sin that can entangle spiritual champions in a constant web of defeat. They have the spiritual power to overcome any sin.

> **Spiritual champions have been freed from *all* sin. There is no sin that can entangle spiritual champions in a constant web of defeat.**

Spiritual champions are dead to self and therefore free from the power of sin. These two realities are possible because of Jesus' death on the cross.

The Enemy of Satan Was Defeated

Satan thought the cross represented a smashing victory over Jesus. There Christ was disgraced before the world. Naked. Hurting. Rejected. Defeated.

But appearances can be deceiving!

The reality was that, on the cross, Jesus disarmed Satan himself and all of his demonic army. Their dictatorship was obliterated, their authority stripped. Jesus publicly disgraced them through the very thing they thought symbolized His defeat. He triumphed over them through the cross!

Satan held the keys to death, the most potent weapon in his arsenal. Yet in His resurrection, the ultimate spiritual champion, Jesus Christ, overcame even death.

That is why spiritual champions have great spiritual authority. Satan has no power over them as long as they abide in Jesus. Not even death can terrorize a spiritual champion, because such a champion knows death is not the end, but the beginning. The end of this life is the beginning of eternal worship of Jesus Christ.

Jesus came to be the ultimate spiritual champion by defeating all of His opponents. Not one of them can even rise in His presence. He has defeated self, sin, and Satan. When He lives in us and is manifested through us, all of our enemies are defeated. This is why we can live like spiritual champions.

Not only did Jesus defeat all His enemies, but He also holds first place in everything.

By Holding First Place in Everything

When the spiritual battles ended, only One figure was left standing on the field. Jesus Christ's defeat of all His enemies elevated Him to first place in everything. Colossians 1:17-18 says,

> And He is before all things, and in him all things hold together. He is also head of the body, the church; and He is the beginning, the first-born from the dead; so that He Himself might come to have first place in everything.

The Lord Jesus Christ has existed eternally. In Him, the whole world is held together. He is the A and the Z, the first and the last. He is also the first one ever to overcome death, hell, and the grave. This is why He has first place in everything.

No place in all the universe exists where Jesus is not in first place. There is no circumstance, situation, or crisis where Jesus is less than number one. Wherever He resides, He is Lord—and He resides everywhere. He has not been in a championship struggle in two thousand years. The cross brought down His enemy publicly.

Jesus Christ is the true champion of the universe. He shares glory with no one. Not even the mightiest angel ever created can compete on the same field with Him. He is superior to all. First. Lord. Champion.

Therefore, in the life of a spiritual champion, Jesus Christ is number one. He is the leader and the Lord of his life.

This means that, since all of the enemies of Jesus are at His feet, they are also at the feet of every spiritual champion. Since Jesus is in first place in everything, He is first place in their lives. A real spiritual champion lives in the grateful knowledge that Jesus has first place in everything. Every decision, every action, every thought, and every word in a spiritual champion's life mirrors the Lordship of Jesus Christ. This is the life of a spiritual champion.

The Eternal Dynasty of Jesus

Unlike human dynasties, the dynasty of Jesus Christ is not limited in duration. It is not hindered by human organization or imperfection. Jesus' dynasty will never change. Even pride will not alter the dynasty of Jesus.

First, the dynasty of Jesus is eternal. Revelation 1:8 tells us, "'I am the

Alpha and the Omega,' says the Lord God, 'who is and who was and who is to come, the Almighty.'"

Jesus existed before anything else was. He is alive today and He will exist forever. He is eternal. Therefore, Jesus' dynasty will be eternal.

Second, the dynasty of Jesus is unchanging. In Hebrews 13:8 we read, "Jesus Christ *is* the same yesterday and today, *yes* and forever."

Jesus never changes. Oh, He changes people. He changes circumstances. But Jesus Himself never changes.

Third, Jesus cannot be defeated. He is God. Not one missile of Satan can come within a galaxy of bringing Him down. The words of an atheist cannot cause Him to shudder. The liberals have never made Him move. Do not ever forget His full name. It is, *Lord* Jesus Christ!

One of the contemporary songs that our choir sings as a call to worship is titled, "Forever King." That is exactly who and what Jesus is. He is forever King. This is why His dynasty is eternal.

Gentlemen, Jesus is the all-time champion. The undisputed champion. The undefeated champion. He is the eternal champion with an eternal dynasty.

Some great things happened to each of us who have embraced Jesus Christ as Lord and Savior. Let me list just a few of them.

You Are on His Team

When you received Christ into your life you became a member of the family of God. Paul tells us in Romans 8:16-17,

> The Spirit Himself bears witness with our spirit that we are children of God, and if children, heirs also, heirs of God and fellow heirs with Christ, if indeed we suffer with *Him* in order that we may also be glorified with *Him*.

You are a child of God. Therefore, you are an heir of God and a fellow-heir of Jesus Christ. You will experience not only His life, but His suffering as well. And one day you will be glorified with Him and will become just like Him.

Think of it: You are on God's team! That means you are on a winning team. God's team never loses; His team has never suffered a defeat. It may look as if God has suffered some major setbacks, but that's impossible. Who can set back the One who's in charge of all things?

> **You are on God's team! That means you are on a winning team. God's team never loses; His team has never suffered a defeat.**

If you have joined God's winning team, you are not moving *toward* spiritual victory, you are moving *from* spiritual victory in every part of your life. That's why you can be a spiritual champion!

You Are as He Is

We are not God. We are not even little gods. But we know God. This has incredible implications for us.

The Bible tells us that "as He is, so also are we in this world" (1 John 4:17). What does that mean?

It means that just as Jesus was victorious in this world, so are we victorious in this world. It means that just as Jesus suffered in this world, so will we suffer in this world. I do not understand all that this means, but I do understand that it is time to discard all of the fleshly, pseudo-spiritual lines such as, "I am just doing the best I can," or "I am going to fail as long as I am here on this earth," or "We are all going to sin continually."

No doubt we will fail. Sin is still possible for us and we need to offer our all to God. But it is time to stop accommodating our sinfulness. It is time we understand that we are as He is in this world. That means victorious. Triumphant. Winning. Successful.

Champions!

Jesus Desires to Make You a Spiritual Champion

Jesus took up your cause while He was here on this earth. He fought for you. He defeated all of His enemies for you. Why was this so important to Him? Because He desired to make you into a spiritual champion.

Without Jesus, we were lost in our sin. Helpless. Hopeless. With Jesus, our sins are forgiven and our lives are filled with meaning and hope. Jesus knew that unless He died for us, we could never become spiritual champions. It was simply beyond our grasp.

Do you realize that the passion which motivated Jesus to die on the cross was His desire to have eternal fellowship with us? Sin had stolen this joy and hope, but Jesus' blood restored both. The Bible says in 2 Corinthians 5:21, "He made Him who knew no sin *to be* sin on our behalf, that we might become the righteousness of God in Him."

> The only ultimate spiritual champion wants us to follow in His footsteps. He beckons us toward the winner's circle and has promised to equip us with everything we need to get there.

Jesus' righteousness covers us and makes it possible for us to become spiritual champions. The only ultimate spiritual champion wants us to follow in His footsteps. He beckons us toward the winner's circle and has promised to equip us with everything we need to get there.

The only question is, will we accept His invitation? Will you?

S T U D Y   Q U E S T I O N S

1. What comes to mind when you think of the term "dynasty"? Have you ever been involved in one? Explain.

2. What is your favorite "dynasty" in sports history? Why? What happened to end its dynasty?

3. How is Jesus the Ultimate Spiritual Champion? What difference does this make to us?

4. Read Colossians 2:13-15. How did Jesus defeat all His opponents? What difference does this make to you?

5. Read Romans 6-7. How does Jesus help us to defeat the enemy of self? Is He doing this in your own experience? If so, how? If not, why not?

6. Read Galatians 2:20. What does Paul say happened to him? Is this true of him alone, or of other Christians as well? Explain.

7. How did Jesus defeat the enemy of sin? If He defeated it, then why do we still have to fight it?

8. How did Jesus defeat the enemy of Satan? What does this mean for us? What will this ultimately mean for Satan?

9. Read Colossians 1:17-18. In what way does Jesus hold first place in everything? Why is this important? How would it change our circumstances if He didn't hold first place in everything?

10. Read Romans 8:16-17. Have you become a member of Jesus' "team"? If so, how? If not, why not?

11. Ronnie says "we are not moving toward spiritual victory, but moving from spiritual victory." What does this mean? How does it affect how we live our lives, day to day?

PART TWO

How to Win It

The Profile of a Spiritual Champion

Perhaps one of the most famous profiles in U.S. history is the gaunt, yet dignified visage of Abraham Lincoln, the sixteenth president of the United States of America. The old photographs we have of Lincoln stare back at us with the face of a sober, somber, and far-seeing man.

Yet not everyone liked his profile. During his embattled presidency of a nation in civil war, a little girl wrote to Mr. Lincoln to give him some advice. She thought he looked much too thin in his newspaper photographs and advised him that he would benefit greatly by growing a beard.

So he did.

And that is why the most famous profiles we have of this most famous man all feature a dignified, close-cropped beard that partially covers (in the mind of a little girl) a too-skinny face.

Famous profiles, like Lincoln's, are easy to identify because they all possess distinctive features that set them apart from others. A good profile highlights these features in a memorable way.

I'd like to take some time right now to design a profile of a real spiritual champion, a profile we can build upon throughout the remainder of the book. Let's look at four memorable features.

Remembers What Made Him a Spiritual Champion

One of the great challenges of a spiritual champion is to remember what made him one. If he fails to remember this, he won't remain a champion for long. Therefore, let's remember what makes anyone into a spiritual champion.

One person and one person

> One of the great challenges of a spiritual champion is to remember what made him one. If he fails to remember this, he won't remain a champion for long.

alone makes a man into a spiritual champion: Jesus Christ. The life that He lived, the death He suffered, and the miracle of His resurrection make it possible for you and I to become spiritual champions.

The moment we forget that Jesus lived a sinless life, died a cruel death for us, and was raised bodily from the dead by the power of God, we become filled with pride and deceive ourselves into thinking it was our own efforts or determination or will power that made us into spiritual champions. That's nonsense. It is Jesus alone who can make us into spiritual champions.

None of us can save ourselves. Jesus is the Savior of the world and spiritual victory is attainable for spiritual champions precisely and only because Jesus defeated all of His opponents. Our abilities and talents do not contribute to spiritual victory. Spiritual victory is not of us, but of Him.

A spiritual champion remembers what made him a spiritual champion in the first place. He saturates his whole life in the person and work of Jesus Christ. Jesus is the one who made us winners!

Reflects on Who He Is as a Spiritual Champion

Reflection and meditation is critical in the life of a spiritual champion. As he thinks about who he is as a spiritual champion, he is empowered to be true to who he is. Personal performance is never what makes a spiritual champion live victoriously. A victorious spiritual life results from knowing his identity in Jesus Christ.

Do you understand who you are in Jesus Christ? So many men do not. They don't expect to be spiritual champions because they have a completely inadequate view of who they are as believers. If they could only begin to grasp the riches they already have in Christ, I'm convinced they would set their sights on becoming a spiritual champion.

So who are you in Christ? Remember, I am talking about who you are *right now*. I am not talking about your future, but your present. When you reflect deeply on the following eleven characteristics, you will see that becoming a spiritual champion is not some far-off, impossible goal, but a natural extension of who you already are in Christ.

Fact #1: You are a transformed person.

One of the most colorful and contributing personalities in the New Testament was a man named Paul. Before his miraculous conversion, his name was Saul. While on his way to Damascus, God cut Saul down to size, changed his life, and later gave him a new name (which means "small").

This astute, intelligent, religious man—who specialized in "Christian-bashing"—was transformed by God. God saved him, changed him, and made him an apostle. Paul's second letter to the church at Corinth proclaims in unmistakable terms a believer's new identity in Christ: "Therefore if anyone is in Christ, *he is* a new creature; the old things passed away; behold, new things have come" (2 Corinthians 5:17).

A believer in Jesus Christ is a transformed person, changed by the power of God. Contrary to today's pop gospel of self and power, none of us can transform ourselves. It took a God-size miracle to accomplish our transformation. But we have been changed! Those who lay hold of this tremendous truth soon find themselves well on their way to becoming spiritual champions.

Fact #2: You are a triumphant person.

The result of a transformed life is that God has made you triumphant. Second Corinthians 2:14 says, "But thanks be to God, who always leads us in His triumph in Christ, and manifests through us the sweet aroma of the knowledge of Him in every place."

How can we always be lead in triumphal procession? What makes this possible? Because we have been transformed into "saints." Don't let that word fool you! There's far more to it than you might think. For example, the Bible says, "Paul, an apostle of Christ Jesus by the will of God, to the saints who are at Ephesus, and who are faithful in Christ Jesus: Grace to you and peace from God our Father and the Lord Jesus Christ" (Ephesians 1:1-2).

What is a saint? A saint is a triumphant person. A saint is not someone who is pious and arrogant. You are a saint because you have been cleansed by the blood of Jesus Christ. You are a saint because you have been changed by Jesus Christ. You are a saint because the Holy Spirit, who now lives in you, is changing you more into the likeness of Jesus Christ every day. Of course, we deserved none of this; it's all a gift of grace. Through grace we are given the power to be saints, to live the Christian life.

You are a saint. You are triumphant. You are a winner. What better start could a spiritual champion get?

Fact #3: You have received a heavenly transfer.

One of the marks of biblical faith is an eagerness to receive God's Word for what it says. It is valid whether we understand it or not. It is God's Word. If we are wise we will receive it and respond to it in faith. God's Word says in Ephesians 1:3, "Blessed be the God and Father of our Lord Jesus Christ, who has blessed us with every spiritual blessing in the heavenly places in Christ."

Note what God says in this verse: All His spiritual blessings are ours! And where will we discover these blessings? In the heavenly places.

Now, I admit I don't understand this fully. Yet by faith, I know I have received a heavenly transfer. And what a transfer it is! God said I have been given *every* spiritual blessing that exists. How many is that? I have no idea. But texts such as Genesis 22:17-18 (cf. Galatians 3:14) suggest that these blessings outnumber the sand on the seashore and the stars in the sky. And what, exactly, are these blessings? Again, I'm not sure. But other texts such as 1 Corinthians 2:9 suggest these staggering blessings are far greater than we could ever conceive or imagine. And they're all ours!

As believers in Jesus Christ, we have dual citizenship. We live physical-

> We live physically on earth but spiritually in heaven. This world is not our home. That's why it's so foolish to drive down stakes on this planet as if we were going to be here forever.

ly on earth but spiritually in heaven. This world is not our home. That's why it's so foolish to drive down stakes on this planet as if we were going to be here forever. We're not, thank God.

Fact #4: You are chosen by God.

One of the greatest mysteries in all of the Bible is that of God's sovereignty and our will to choose. John MacArthur advised me to teach both truths with equal zeal. As people hear the whole Word of God, in time the balance will come.

Ephesians 1:4 highlights one side of this tremendous mystery: "Just as He chose us in Him before the foundation of the world, that we should be holy and blameless before Him."

God sovereignly chose you, apart from anything you would do or have done. He is the Author of your salvation from beginning to end. He chose you before the beginning of all time for the purpose of making you more like Jesus Christ.

Men, we are chosen by God! The same God who chose us in salvation will not let us falter aimlessly through this life. We have purpose. We have direction. We have a destiny. We are fully equipped to become the spiritual champions God meant for us to be.

Fact #5: You are adopted into God's family.

Many men I know seem to lack the confidence and security they need to move through life with boldness and strength. Ephesians 1:4-5 should encourage such men: "In love He predestined us to adoption as sons through Jesus Christ to Himself, according to the kind intention of His will."

If this doesn't give us great confidence, what will? Before the beginning of all time, God placed His loving mark on us. He adopted us into the family of God, not as some pitiable, wretched waifs, but as co-heirs with Christ. Just as in Roman law, God's adopted children have the same rights and privileges as biological children. With a dad like Almighty God, how can we lose?

Our confidence is in Christ. Our security is in Christ. We are adopted into the family of God. What an overwhelming spiritual blessing!

Fact #6: You are fully accepted by God.

Even though none of us deserve complete acceptance by a holy and righteous God, we have it. Paul tells us in Romans 15:16 that through God's grace we have become "acceptable to God, sanctified by the Holy Spirit" (NIV). Ephesians 1:6 tells us that His grace was "freely bestowed on us in the Beloved."

Our acceptance is based on God's grace, which is bestowed upon us freely in Jesus. It wasn't coerced, it wasn't earned, and it wasn't a reward for good behavior. Our acceptance by God has nothing to do with our performance or what others may think of us. We are completely accepted by God because of Jesus. Since it was so freely given, there's nothing we have to do to get it or keep it. *Already* we have been fully accepted by God.

Fact #7: You are redeemed.

Before Christ, sin owned us. We were in bondage to it. Death was the necessary consequence of our sin. If we were to escape this consequence, someone would have to pay the price for sin. The Bible says in Ephesians 1:7-8, "In Him we have redemption through His blood, the forgiveness of our trespasses, according to the riches of His grace, which He lavished upon us."

Jesus Christ paid a ransom for our sin. It was a very high price indeed. Yet when Jesus died in our place, this price was paid in full and we were released from our bondage to sin. We were freed from our slavery to sin and death.

If you have named Jesus as your Lord and Savior, you have been set free by the blood of Jesus. You have been released from the power of sin. Sin is no longer your master; you are no longer a slave to sin. Instead, you are now a slave to righteousness. This is the stuff of which spiritual champions are made!

Fact #8: You are forgiven.

When you were redeemed by Jesus Christ, you were also forgiven by Him. Your sins were carried or sent away. You were granted a pardon for all of your sins—past, present, and future.

One of the great consequences of this complete forgiveness is that there is no reason to feel guilty anymore! You do not have to carry your sins on your back like a knapsack. Jesus has carried all your sins away. The burden and guilt of all your sins were carried by Him on the cross. He did this so you would not have to carry them around with you.

Men, you are forgiven. This is who you are in Christ.

Fact #9: You are a receiver of God's mysteries.

People love to purchase and read books of mysteries. Did you know the Bible says you are a receiver of the mysteries of God? Ephesians 1:8-10 says,

In all wisdom and insight He made known to us the mystery of His will, according to His kind intention which He purposed in Him with a view to an administration suitable to the fulness of the times, that is, the summing up of all things in Christ, things in the heavens and things upon the earth.

This scriptural "mystery" refers to a sacred secret or to something now known that was once hidden.

The mystery which has been given to us is that God will one day bring all things in heaven and on earth together under one Head, the Lord Jesus Christ. We can know, with confidence, that this world is moving toward the day when everything will be placed under the authority of Jesus Christ. We have been given wisdom by God to see this and other mysteries.

Fact #10: You are a receiver of God's inheritance.

God Himself is the source of your inheritance. All that is His is yours as well. But not only do you *have* God's inheritance, you *are* God's inheritance! The Bible says in Ephesians 1:10-12,

In Him also we have obtained an inheritance, having been predestined according to His purpose who works all things after the counsel of His will, to the end that we who were the first to hope in Christ should be to the praise of His glory.

In Jesus, you are a receiver of God's inheritance. Paul informed us in Romans 8:16,17 that "the Spirit Himself bears witness with our spirit that we are children of God, and if children, heirs also, heirs of God and fellow heirs with Christ."

Just imagine: Everything Jesus has is yours! There's no reason to wallow in the "poor-me's." All God has is yours. And even greater than this miracle, you are *His* inheritance. God values you beyond imagination. He loves you and accepts you fully.

This, gentlemen, is who you are in Jesus Christ!

Fact #11: You are sealed with the Holy Spirit.

A seal on a letter or contract has always been used as a mark of identification. The Bible says you were sealed with the Holy Spirit. Ephesians 1:13-14 informs us,

In Him, you also, after listening to the message of truth, the gospel of your salvation—having also believed, you were sealed in Him with the Holy Spirit of promise, who is given as a pledge of our inheritance, with a view to the redemption of God's own possession, to the praise of His glory.

The Holy Spirit is given to every person who receives salvation. He is our seal and the pledge of our inheritance.

To be sealed with the Holy Spirit means that God owns us. He has tagged us for Himself and attached His seal of ownership upon our lives. The sealing of the Spirit also means that God protects us. We are protected and secure until Jesus comes again. The Spirit is also a pledge given as a deposit to guarantee our future inheritance.

> **"** How we live will flow from the knowledge of who we are. No one ever became a spiritual champion without reflecting upon who he is in Jesus Christ. **"**

Can you believe this? God owns us. God protects us. God secures us. God is promising us a future inheritance. All these things belong to us *right now*. They are what enable us to become true spiritual champions.

These eleven truths are crucial to our spiritual lives. We must understand who we are in Jesus Christ.

How we live will flow from the knowledge of who we are. No one ever became a spiritual champion without reflecting upon who he is in Jesus Christ. It's an essential prerequisite.

Resolves to Have the Right Priorities

The third major distinctive of a spiritual champion is that he resolves to live by the right priorities.

The first priority of a spiritual champion, of course, is Jesus Christ. Central to the life of a spiritual champion is his relationship with Jesus.

Spiritual champions know that when Jesus Christ is not the priority in their lives, they open themselves up to sin. They open the door to continual failure. The inevitable result is discouragement and frustration, and no spiritual champion wants to make this ugly pair his constant companions.

In the life of a spiritual champion, Jesus Christ is first and central in everything. Anything other than this demeans Christ and demeans him. On the other hand, spiritual champions know that success will come to the man who places Christ first and central in everything.

Realizes the Dimension of His Influence

The final distinctive of a spiritual champion is that he knows and appreciates how large his influence can be. He knows that, even when it doesn't appear to be true, his life and attitudes and actions are having a major effect on those with whom he comes into contact.

A spiritual champion has a sense of destiny in his life, not for personal grandeur, but for the welfare of others. A real spiritual champion understands that God wants to use him in a very influential manner. When a spiritual champion understands his destiny, this dimension can grow to be "God-size."

If you are a believer, God already has done a great work in your life. He has not done this so that you can hoard it, but so that you can share it with others. Spiritual champions realize that God wants to use their influence for the benefit of others. This is leadership.

Spiritual champions are leaders for God and God uses them in a great way to influence many other people for Him. A real spiritual champion realizes the dimension of his influence.

These four principles apply not only to the spiritual realm, but to many dimensions of life. For example, a champion in business jeopardizes his successful status anytime he forgets what made him a champion, who he is as a champion, if he fails to maintain the proper priorities that made him a champion, and if he forgets the influence he has upon others as a champion.

So what does this look like? How does a real-life spiritual champion act? Let me introduce you to George Hawk, an ordinary guy who found himself in a soldier's uniform in the middle of what we call World War II.

George found himself slowly drifting to earth one day when he was shot down over Anzio, Italy. Held as a prisoner of war for fifteen months, George was brutally tortured and his six-foot-two-inch frame shrank from 215 pounds to a little over 120. He watched his companions die. Very quickly all the "usual" measurements of success dropped away and his survival instinct kicked into full gear. George Hawk was an ordinary man in many respects— except one. He was a great man of faith.

While others around him descended into animal-like savagery, George's faith gave him extraordinary peace. In the midst of his brutal captivity he wrote a moving prayer, which eventually was read at his memorial service after his death. That prayer read:

> Oh, God, my Creator and Protector, I know that you are near me. So I adore Thee, body and soul, with complete submission to Thy will.
>
> Thou hast saved me from death, which has overtaken my companions, and have permitted that I be a prisoner. I will bear patiently and hopefully the difficulties of my state.
>
> Bless me and my companions here. Grant us to live in peace, comforting and consoling one another with fraternal love and charity.
>
> Bless my family, who are far away, my friends and all I love, my country and my comrades in arms.
>
> Give me peace and protect me from despair and melancholy and, above all, keep me from offending Thee. Keep me rejoicing in hope, patient in tribulation and constant in prayer. Amen.

George Hawk didn't liberate Italy. He didn't fall on a grenade or save a thousand soldiers with a rusty old carbine or drive Hitler to his knees. He spent much of the war as a captive of Axis forces—but he remained a spiritual champion the whole time. And even now he's standing tall in the champion's circle in heaven.

How did he do it? The same way any of us must do it. If you or I hope to be God's man, a Jesus man, then we must remember what Jesus did for us, understand fully who we are in Jesus, resolve to make Jesus first and central in our lives, and realize that God wants to use us. This is the profile of a real spiritual champion.

The Two Anchors of a Spiritual Champion

In a traditional shopping mall there are at least two anchor stores. Usually these stores are part of a major chain such as Macy's, Sears, or J. C. Penney's. In between these two anchor stores are scores of other specialty shops such as shoe stores, clothing stores, and many times even a Christian bookstore.

All of these stores together provide the synergy that makes the mall successful. The success of one usually increases the success of others. Yet their influence is not identical. The anchor stores are more vital to the success of the mall than the specialty stores. They provide the stability that enables the mall to achieve a certain level of success; that's why they're called "anchor stores."

In the same way that a mall uses two anchor stores to achieve success in business, a spiritual champion uses two anchor texts to achieve success in life. He knows that if he makes liberal use of these two anchors, he will enjoy stability and growth in his Christian walk. As he walks through the years, he knows it is necessary to know where he is in order to get to where he wants to go. These two anchors are his directional checks for the rest of his life.

"8:37 Check"

The first anchor in the life of a spiritual champion is found in Romans 8:37: "But in all these things we overwhelmingly conquer through Him who loved us."

The word "conquer" here means to win a victory. Through Jesus Christ, we have won. Through every challenge, difficult circumstance, or unfortunate situation, we can overwhelmingly conquer through Jesus Christ. Regardless of the storms that may sweep over us in life, the truth of this verse can anchor us in Jesus Christ.

I encourage you to periodically give yourself an "8:37 check." I do this myself, and it works. Ask yourself, "Am I living like a conqueror? Am I being an anchor in the midst of the storm? Am I walking on my difficulties, or are they walking on me?" Remember, you don't triumph on your own. You don't conquer through your own brute strength or through the iron determination of your own will. The verse says, "In all these things we overwhelmingly conquer *through Him who loved us*." This 8:37 check isn't an invitation to suck it up and grit it out; it's a challenge to remember who you are in Christ and what you have in Him. You'll remain victorious only so long as you remember that He won the battle, not you.

When you're comfortable giving yourself an 8:37 check, why not give your Christian buddies an 8:37 check, as well? You might say to them, "Remember 8:37" or "Read 8:37" or "What you need is 8:37." When they ask you what you mean, refer to Romans 8:37 and encourage them to become spiritual champions themselves.

I know this might seem a little odd at first; but spiritual champions know they can't stand strong on their own. They need to give and receive all the encouragement that's available. The 8:37 check is a simple, effective way to tap into such encouragement.

"4:13 Check"

The second anchor in the life of a spiritual champion is Philippians 4:13, a verse we briefly considered before. It says, "I can do all things through Him who strengthens me."

The Bible says that we can do all things through the power of God. He is able to strengthen us through everything we face in life.

This is great news, but don't miss the essential part of this verse. It doesn't talk about what I can do, but what God does through me. It isn't my strength, but His.

Years ago I introduced my boys to this 4:13 check. Today when they are in athletic competition I may yell to them "4:13." They know what I mean. I am calling them to depend on God's strength. My son Nicholas placed "4:13" on his All-Star cap as a reminder to him.

In this world full of negativism, criticism, and pessimism, we need to be reminded frequently of Philippians 4:13. When you're discouraged, give yourself a 4:13 check. When one of your friends needs encouragement, give him a 4:13—remembering, of course, that it's not a cattle prod, but a royal invitation to dine at the table of the King of kings.

A real spiritual champion is fully aware of what God wants to do through him. In all circumstances he carries the confidence of Romans 8:37 and Philippians 4:13. That doesn't mean he sails through life unaffected by pain or suffering or unexpected setbacks, but that through it all he never forgets God has made him a winner and a champion.

> 66
>
> Spiritual champions know they're not moving *toward* victory, but *from* victory. Their greatest challenge is to live up to what God says they already are in Jesus Christ.
>
> 99

Spiritual champions know they're not moving *toward* victory, but *from* victory. They are winners. Their greatest challenge is to live up to what God says they already are in Jesus Christ. They are conquerors in Jesus. They can do all things through Jesus. They are "Jesus men." They are real spiritual champions because they believe it, think like it, and live like it.

That's the challenge I want to lay before you in the rest of this book. God is calling you to be a spiritual champion—not an insufferable, holier-than-thou spiritual bigot, but a man who has decided to "go for it" with God and for his family. A man who is not satisfied with going through the motions, with doing the bare minimum, with the lowest common denominator. I want to challenge you to be great for God—*not* based on fleshly effort and *not* as a way to earn approval, but, in Paul's words, "to run in such a way to win the prize."

The prize is out there and it has your name on it. Yet if you want it, you have to run in such a way to win it. Remember, it isn't given to everybody who suits up. Only those who choose to be champions, who train to win, who play by the rules and who finish strong, ever step into the winner's circle. You can be one of them. And you can start right now.

S T U D Y   Q U E S T I O N S

1. Other than Abraham Lincoln's, what is the most famous profile you can think of? Describe it. What's so memorable about it?

2. Do you consider yourself a spiritual champion? Why or why not?

3. When a spiritual champion reflects on how he became what he is, what does he think about?

4. Discuss each of the following attributes of a spiritual champion. What does each mean in general, and what does it mean to you in particular?

A. A transformed person (2 Corinthians 5:17)

B. A triumphant person (2 Corinthians 2:14)

C. Has received a heavenly transfer (Ephesians 1:3)

D. Has been chosen by God (Ephesians 1:4)

E. Has been adopted into God's family (Ephesians 1:4-5)

F. Has been fully accepted by God (Ephesians 1:6)

G. Was redeemed (Ephesians 1:7-8)

H. Has been forgiven (Ephesians 1:7)

I. Has received God's mysteries (Ephesians 1:8-10)

J. Has received God's inheritance (Ephesians 1:10-12; Romans 8:16,17)

K. Is sealed with the Holy Spirit (Ephesians 1:13-14)

5. What are the "right" priorities of a spiritual champion? Why are these the "right" ones? Are they yours? Explain.

6. Try to describe the dimensions of your influence. Who do you influence? How do you influence them?

7. Read Romans 8:37. In what way is this verse a helpful "anchor" for navigating the storms of life?

8. Read Philippians 4:13. In what way is this verse a helpful "anchor" for navigating the storms of life?

C H A P T E R   F O U R

The Passion of a Spiritual Champion

Corporate America has been changed radically by the leading retail firm in the country. You guessed it. Wal-Mart. It is hard to believe that this mega-corporation had its humble beginning in Bentonville, Arkansas, in 1950. Back then it was called Walton's Five and Dime.

Anticipating that the future of retail was in the discount concept, the first Wal-Mart store opened on July 2, 1962, in Rogers, Arkansas. In the first year, the Rogers store did $1 million in business. The multi-billion-dollar business called Wal-Mart had begun.

What was the key to this retail phenomenon? A man with passion named Sam Walton. Sam had a passion to win. In his own words, "I have always pursued everything I was interested in with a true passion—some would call obsession—to win."[1] His passion not only created the greatest retail business in America, but also kept it number one throughout his lifetime. Even though Sam Walton is deceased, his passion still provides the motivation for this business today.

It has been no secret to those of us who live within minutes of Wal-Mart headquarters that those associated with this retailer attend a 7:30 A.M. meeting every Saturday morning. Many times Walton's passion would awaken these fellow-workers with the Hog call—the University of Arkansas cheer:

Whoooooooooooooooooooooo Pig Sooey!
Whoooooooooooooooooooooooooo Pig Sooey!
Whoooooooooooooooooooooooooooooooo Pig Sooey!
Razorbacks!

Just because they were in a business meeting, Walton thought, did not mean it had to be dull and serious.

When Walton visited various stores across the country, inevitably he would lead the employees in his own Wal-Mart cheer:

> Give me a W! Give an A! Give me an L! Give me a squiggly! (Here, everybody sort of does the twist.) Give me an M! Give me an A! Give me an R! Give me a T! What's that spell? Walmart! What that's spell? Walmart! Who's No. 1? THE CUSTOMER![2]

Sam Walton's passionate life refused to let business go as normal. He knew if he could make work fun and shopping unique, he could build a great company.

Walton's passion made him the wealthiest man in the world. It was not wealth, however, which drove him, but the competition. He got up every morning with a passion to make a difference with his life. Walton also desired to make a difference in the lives of his employees. This is why even in the 1950s he was sharing information and profit with his employees.

On October 1, 1970, Sam Walton took the company public. If a person had purchased 100 shares of stock in that original offering, he would have spent $1,650. By 1992, he would have enjoyed nine two-for-one splits resulting in 51,200 shares. At $60 per share in 1992, that original $1,650 investment would have been worth $3 million!

Walton's passion motivated him to keep the customer in the right place: number one. One of his senior vice-presidents tells an interesting story about how Wal-Mart's "people greeters" got their start:

> Let me tell you how Wal-Mart came to have people greeters. Back in 1980, Mr. Walton and I went into a Wal-Mart in Crowley, La. The first thing we saw was this older gentleman standing there. The man didn't know me, and didn't see Sam, but he said, "Hi! How are ya? Glad you're here. If there's anything I can tell you about our store, just let me know." Neither Sam nor I had ever seen such a thing. The store, it turned out, had had trouble with shoplifting. Its manager didn't want to intimidate the honest customers by posting a guard, but he wanted to leave a clear message that if you stole, someone was there who would see it.
>
> Well, Sam thought that was the greatest idea he'd ever heard of. We put greeters at the front of every single store. I guess his vindication was that in 1989 he walked into a K-Mart in Illinois and found that they had installed people greeters at their front doors.[3]

The passion of Sam Walton always placed the customer first. This strategy explains why the company still reigns as champion in the retail business today.

Each June thousands of people converge on Northwest Arkansas to be a part of Wal-Mart's annual stockholders' meeting. The meeting does not take place in a somber environment like a large conference room or banquet hall, but in Bud Walton Arena, home of the University of Arkansas Razorback basketball team. The arena overflows with up to twenty thousand people in attendance. It's not a meeting so much as an event. It is still driven with the passion of Sam Walton, with all the excitement of a group of college cheerleaders leading fans at a Saturday afternoon game.

Passion is contagious. Families catch it. Churches catch it. Organizations catch it. Even businesses catch it. In 1991, the chief executive officer for General Electric, Jack Welch, made the following comments after being a part of Wal-Mart's shareholders' meeting on three occasions:

> **Passion is contagious. Families catch it. Churches catch it. Organizations catch it. Even businesses catch it.**

> Everybody there has a passion for an idea, and everyone's ideas count. Hierarchy doesn't matter. They get 80 people in a room and understand how to deal with each other without structure. I have been there three times now. Every time you go to that place in Arkansas, you can fly back to New York without a plane. The place actually vibrates.[4]

The life of Sam Walton infused passion into some of the great business leaders of our time. His passion created a "can do" spirit in people.

I never had the privilege of meeting Sam Walton, though I really would have loved to. I watched his memorial service in April 1992 on television like thousands of others in Northwest Arkansas. People who did know him have told me he was definitely a believer and follower of Jesus Christ, and that he was just as passionate in his faith as he was in business.

I cannot tell you first-hand the measure of passion for God Sam Walton had, but then again, I don't need to. This book is not about Sam Walton; it is about us. It is about our passion for God. If each of us could be as passionate about God as we are about other things, we couldn't help but become the spiritual champions God is calling us to be.

As a spiritual champion, passion has to be a major part of our lives. Are you a man of passion? I am not talking about passion as it is defined by the polluted standards of Hollywood. I am talking about your being a man who is filled with a passion for Jesus Christ.

What Passion Is Not

Sometimes it is easier to define a word by contrasting it to what it is not. Let's follow this road for awhile and see if we can successfully define the word "passion."

Passion is not sensuality.

Hollywood has had a catastrophic influence upon our contemporary culture. The movie and video industry has raped our nation of its innocence. It has destroyed virtuous minds. It has devastated families. It has ravaged the lives of countless individuals.

The advertising and marketing industry has contributed to this moral slide. Beautiful, half-dressed women are paraded seductively before a gaping male audience to advertise products of all kinds from shaving cream to alkaline batteries. The images are omnipresent and unavoidable. You see them piped into your home through television or splashed on glossy magazine pages or pasted to gigantic billboards along the interstate.

What are these advertisers doing? Is there really a connection between sultry, curvaceous models and a certain brand of multi-grain bread? Hardly, and the advertisers know it. They're simply going for our pocketbooks through our mind. They are fully aware that if they can draw us in sensually, they can draw us to buy their products.

Sensuality degenerates the mind of a man. It degrades the meaning of the word "passion." It degrades the meaning of a man.

Most men are biting on the lure of late-night television, adult-only movies, and cable channels because they are driven to fulfill the lusts that sensuality has created within them. Some men have fed their lusts since boyhood through exposure to this kind of filth, beginning with some kind of cheap pornographic literature. What most of us fail to realize is that everything we put into our mind, we will have to deal with at some point in our life. What can you say to your twelve-year-old son when you confront him about watching a dirty movie and he replies, "But dad, didn't you rent this one just last week?"

If a man watches or reads sensual material, he forfeits his opportunity to be the spiritual champion God wants Him to be for his family. When a man permits his children to watch sensual prime-time television shows, he is opening their minds to Satan, the porno king. Do not be fooled. Whatever is placed into your mind or the minds of your children will have to be dealt with not only for the rest of your life, but theirs, too.

Spiritual champions do not find their identity in sensuality. They do not fulfill the lusts of our flesh. They say NO to all sensuality. A brief "yes" to even a little of such false passion will open wide the gates of hell into our minds. And we can't afford that.

Passion is not sex.

Passion is often interpreted as a synonym for sex. Our culture takes this as a given, that sexual intercourse has no bounds or limitations. It teaches that sex is open and free to all. Many regard sex as a god or goddess; you can tell by the way they worship it.

While the Bible teaches us that sex is a wonderful gift from God, it also insists that it is not to be experienced by anyone outside the bonds of marriage. This means that sex prior to marriage is unacceptable. It also means that sex outside of marriage is unacceptable.

The act of sex is to be enjoyed by two people from the opposite sex. All sex between two people of the same sex is wrong. Our children and grandchildren will struggle with a clear understanding of their sexuality as long as Christian men simply wink at homosexuality. "Gay pride" is not only an embarrassment to America, but most of all, a terrible sin against God.

A man will find his meaning in life only when he is submissive to God concerning His Laws relating to sexuality. A real man does not have to prove his manhood by playing outside the rules. A spiritual champion knows that if he plays now, he will pay later. He is too wise to buy into the lie that passion is sex.

Passion is not success.

Most men have an insatiable desire for success, despite the fact that it is so ill-defined in our culture. Too often it is equated with houses, cars, land, toys, and money. Many men spend the vast majority of their lives climbing a ladder that never gets them to their desired destination—fulfillment. Inevitably, they have the wrong ladder or the ladder simply breaks. "Wipe-out" is the end result. Sometimes they lose their families. At times, their careers. Not infrequently, their own lives.

Passion is not "success."

A spiritual champion understands the importance of having a right, biblical definition of success. He knows that pursuing the success God describes is more important than the worship of the god our culture calls success. This puny god is not a friend to be embraced; it is an enemy to a spiritual champion.

So what is passion, then? If it is not sensuality, sex, or success, what is it? If fulfillment doesn't come through these false avenues, where is it to be found? What kind of passion lights the fires of a true spiritual champion?

What Passion Is

First, let me reiterate that there is nothing wrong with the word or the emotion of passion. In fact, it needs to describe the life of all spiritual champions. Yet the object of our passion is never to be sensuality, sex, or success. While the world worships them, they are puny and impotent deities. The object of our passion must be Jesus Christ and His kingdom. That naturally brings up the question, what kind of passion is this?

Passion is an emotion.

I live within fifteen minutes of the University of Arkansas. I enjoy visiting Razorback Stadium, located in the beautiful Ozark Mountains. Thousands of people converge there every fall to watch the fighting Razorbacks. We wear our "red and white." We yell, clap, and scream for our team. We second guess the coaching staff as if the decisions depended on us. We are exhausted after the games because we have expended 100 percent of our emotional energy.

As excited as I get about football, however, many men can live without it. Instead, they spend their emotional energy in other sports such as fishing or hunting, or they direct their energy into taking care of their lawns or finishing a home project. The point is, most men can get passionate about some wholesome activity outside of work. There is nothing wrong with being emotional about any of these things. As long as they don't control our lives, they can all be good, healthy, and right.

So why don't we get just as emotional about our faith in Jesus Christ? Why is it that so few men seem to get passionate about their Lord? One reason is that some men view their Christian lives as something not to get emotional or passionate about. It's too private. It's between them and the Lord. At home. Alone.

This is sad. We are emotional beings designed to express those emotions, *especially* in the areas of our lives that mean the most to us.

Gene Layman is a very successful businessman, a leader in his community as well as in his church. Gene also is one of the greatest men of prayer and faith that I have ever known. Yet his stature as a leader never inhibits him from passionately displaying his emotions for God and his faith. His eyes well up with tears as he shares a fervent prayer request. With news of some victory, his body rocks with infectious and unbridled joy. He laughs, he smiles, he mourns, he weeps. His emotion is never sappy, but deeply touching. It makes him approachable and inspires others to feel deeply and to make themselves "touchable." Gene is a man's man, but he is also a deeply emotional man.

> Spiritual champions are men of passion. Their passion wells up inside them out of their genuine gratitude for and appreciation of their Lord. It's a natural part of who they are.

Spiritual champions are emotional men, men of passion. Their passion is not gratuitous, but wells up inside them out of their genuine gratitude for and appreciation of their Lord. It's a natural part of who they are, and it grows as they continue to mature in Christ.

Passion is enthusiasm.

The word enthusiasm comes from two Greek words that mean, "in God" (*en theos*). Enthusiasm is a God-given emotion meant to be expressed toward Him. Because He is the greatest person in the universe, our enthusiasm should be greatest for Him. This is why God could command us, "You shall love the LORD your God with all your heart and with all your soul and with all your might" (Deuteronomy 6:5). It's also why Jesus repeated and even heightened this command in Mark 12:30 when He told us to "love the LORD your God with all your heart, and with all your soul, and with all your mind, and with all your strength."

That's a lot of enthusiasm!

When we are filled with enthusiasm we are filled with excitement, desire, and fire. Each of these words denote a different aspect of the word "passion." Passion is enthusiasm, excitement, desire, and fire. Such expressions of emotion have been given to you by God to be expressed for Him. This does not, of course, mean they shouldn't be expressed for other things; but our primary enthusiasm should be expressed for God.

It saddens me that many men think they are too cool to be enthusiastic for Jesus Christ. While they can get excited about looking at another man's wife or seeing some sex flick or making money on a big deal or showing their new toy to their male friends or acting like a wild man at a sporting event, they sit stone-faced and unmoved in a worship service designed to lift their eyes in wonder and adoration to the King of the universe. They never know what they are missing.

Real spiritual champions are not these kind of men. They are men filled with enthusiasm, excitement, desire, and fire for Jesus Christ. They are so free, so confident, that they can express their passion for God anytime, anywhere, in front of anyone. It's not a show and it's not a front. They can't help it! They do not view their expressions of passion for God as a radical departure from real life, but as the normal Christian life. They fellowship with, worship, and experience Jesus Christ wherever they are. They realize that they exchanged their bondage to sin for freedom at the cross of Jesus Christ, and the natural result is a joyful, powerful, free, passionate expression of love. They wouldn't have it any other way.

How about you? Are you enslaved to what others think about you, or are you free to express your gratitude and thanksgiving to God in a masculine, passionate way? If you're not free but would like to be, let me encourage you to pause right now and ask God to set you free from this bondage. Ask Him to light a fuse in you for Him that can never be put out. Then enjoy the fireworks!

Spiritual champions are free men of great passion, emotion, enthusiasm, excitement, desire, and fire. Just think what would happen in churches if men began to funnel these emotions to Jesus! It could begin to blow the trumpet that would call America to spiritual awakening.

What to Be Passionate About

I'm convinced that unchurched men would become interested in the things of God if they witnessed Christian men who had a deep, abiding passion for Jesus Christ. No one is drawn to half-heartedness or a mediocre faith. Certainly Albert Einstein wasn't.

Charles Misner, an expert in the

> " I'm convinced that unchurched men would become interested in the things of God if they witnessed Christian men who had a deep, abiding passion for Jesus Christ. "

theory of general relativity, guessed that Einstein had little time for the church because of the passionless worship he saw going on there:

> The design of the universe . . . is very magnificent and shouldn't be taken for granted. In fact, I believe that is why Einstein had so little use for organized religion, although he strikes me as a basically very religious man. He must have looked at what the preachers said about God and felt that they were blaspheming. He had seen much more majesty than they had ever imagined, and they were just not talking about the real thing. My guess is that he simply felt that religions he'd run across did not have proper respect . . . for the author of the universe.[5]

Unchurched men are no more interested in religion than you are. Spiritual champions are men of passion. We are to be men who get passionate about Jesus Christ.

But this passion doesn't materialize out of thin air. You don't become passionate about something just because you think you ought to be. Passion for Christ is nurtured the same way any other passion is. And how is that? By spending time with the object of the passion. By gaining a greater and broader and deeper appreciation for it by becoming personally involved.

To fire our passion for Jesus Christ requires this same personal involvement. While there are many ways to do this, let's focus briefly on one of the most important. While I'm sure it won't be a surprise to you, it's extraordinarily important. If you want to be a spiritual champion, you must become increasingly passionate about Jesus Christ. Such passion grows only when you spend time with Him. And that takes meeting with Him regularly.

A Daily Time with God

Your Christian life will never be any greater than your daily time with God. Passion for God simply will not grow without spending significant time with God. That's just the way we're built.

Why is a daily time with God important? A daily time with God gets you in touch with Him. It allows you to experience Him. It sets your life in order. It enables you to live the Spirit-controlled life. It empowers you to be the kind of husband and father you want to be. It will make you more successful in your occupation than you would ever be without it. And it will help you become the spiritual champion God wants you to be.

Nothing will affect your life more than a daily time with God. Neither a positive thinking tape series, the latest best-seller, exercise, a friendship, a good personal disci-

> *Nothing* will affect your life more than a daily time with God. Whenever you genuinely encounter God over a long period of time, you are changed forever.

pline, nor anything else will have the positive effect on your life that a daily time with God will. Whenever you genuinely encounter God over a long period of time, you are changed forever.

Whether you schedule this daily time with God in the morning or evening is not important. What is crucial is that you have it daily and it is quality time with God. I prefer to begin my day with this appointment with God. That way I'm prepared for everything that follows, even the unexpected.

Our goal in this time must always be to meet God, to spend time with Him. It is not to finish a routine or to fulfill the latest growth plan. The goal of a daily time with God is to meet Him. It's of course true that not all such times will "feel" productive. Some days your feelings will tell you that it's all a waste of time. But I beg you, don't let this stop you! Those "dry" times are often the very times that mean the most. Apparent barrenness does not mean failure or uselessness. God will honor your consistency.

Although some people regard daily time with God as a quiet time, I'd advise against making it too quiet. Our desire is that God speaks to us consistently, clearly, and profoundly. The environment needs to be quiet, but not the experience. The experience of our daily time with God needs to be filled with interaction and fellowship between us and God.

Prayer is an essential component of this daily time with God. Without it you cannot fire your passion for God. Prayer is simply talking with God. It is personal dialogue between you and Him. Prayer involves sharing your heart with God. God wants to hear from you, so tell Him of your struggles, your challenges, your victories, and your hopes. The more you do so, the more passionate you'll become about the One to whom you pray.

The Bible is another essential component of becoming passionate for Christ. The Bible is God's means of speaking to us. It contains His personal love letters to us, especially penned to you and I. They are for our life. We're wise if we read the Bible daily. To get the most out of its wisdom, we should study it, meditate upon it, and memorize it. That may sound like a lot of work, but believe me, the rewards far outweigh the costs. We'll never know about that, however, unless we try it out for ourselves.

Yet another important component of this daily time with God, I believe, is keeping a spiritual journal. This journal is nothing more than a letter written to God about what is on your heart. It documents your walk with Jesus Christ. Not only does it get filled with requests to God, but it also records thanksgiving to God when He answers your prayers.[6]

Spiritual champions are passionate about their Lord because they spend consistent and quality time with Him. They know they cannot be successful spiritually and practically without it. Once a man has tasted this kind of rich time with God, he will never be satisfied without it. His passion for God grows along with his commitment to meet with God. And that kind of godly passion draws others like a magnet.

How Passionate Are You?

On a scale of one to ten, with one being "little" and ten being "great," how would you evaluate your passion for Christ? What kind of passion do you have for meeting daily with God? How passionate, excited, enthusiastic, emotional, desirous, and full of fire are you about this crucial area of life?

If only we had the passion in our spiritual lives that Sam Walton had in building Wal-Mart! If only we had the passion in our spiritual lives that we have to improve our golf score, to get our lawn and landscaping manicured perfectly, to make money, to be accepted by our peers, to be recognized as a success in our profession, to kill the ultimate prey in our hunting adventures, to follow our favorite sports team, or to enjoy our favorite recreational or leisure activity! If only we were as passionate for God as we are for all of the other things in His world!

The good news is, we can have such passion. But we have to want it. We have to choose it. We have to go after it, not in the flesh, but in the power of God's Spirit. Then God will provide the means for us to become the fathers we have always wanted to be and the husbands we should have been since the day we were married. Then our great God will delightedly give us all the wisdom to choose the right priorities and to live them out.

> Passion for God is what keeps the work of God going within us and through us. This is the engine that drives a true spiritual champion.

Passion for God is where it all begins. Passion for God is what keeps the work of God going within us and through us. Passion for God allows God to be Himself in us and through us at all times and in all places and in front of all people.

This is the engine that drives a true spiritual champion. This is where true fulfillment and satisfaction are to be found. And this is what it means to be a man.

S T U D Y   Q U E S T I O N S

1. What are you passionate about? What do you wish you were passionate about, but aren't? Explain.

2. Our culture says passion is sensuality. Do you agree? Why or why not?

3. Why does Ronnie say that passion is not sex?

4. Who do you know who is passionate about success? What has this passion caused this person to do (or not do)?

5. Do you find it hard or easy to express emotion? When you get passionate about something, do people see your emotion? Explain.

6. Read Deuteronomy 6:5 and Mark 12:30. What does enthusiasm have to do with passion? What are you enthusiastic about?

7. How much time do you spend with Jesus in the average week? How does this relate to your passion for Him?

8. Ronnie mentions three keys to a daily time with God. How much time do you spend in all three, and how do you think your habits affect your relationship with God?

A. Prayer

B. Bible reading

C. Keeping a spiritual journal

9. On a scale of one to ten, with one being "little" and ten being "great," how passionate are you about Christ? Are you satisfied with this? Explain.

10. Discuss the following sentence: "Passion for God is the engine that drives a true spiritual champion." Do you agree or disagree? Explain.

CHAPTER FIVE

The Priorities of a Spiritual Champion

Y ou see the company's red, white, and blue sign on the tops of cars everywhere you go. Its outlets seem omnipresent. Within minutes of placing your order, its product is delivered. Chances are, most of you have partaken of its offerings more than once. Some of you may have eaten a whole one all by yourselves.

This company was the first to offer fast delivery of its product. Its success came quickly as a result of speed and quality. It seemed unbeatable and unstoppable. At least, it seemed so to its founder and 97 percent owner, Thomas S. Monaghan. Who could possibly stop the juggernaut of Domino's Pizza?

From Success to Disaster and Back Again

Domino's is a tremendous story of success, distractions, and priorities. Monaghan and his brother borrowed $900 to start this business. Within months, their company began to achieve some success. Monaghan targeted collegiate towns in New England and Domino's Pizza grew so rapidly that in 1985, the company opened nine hundred stores—the most a restaurant chain had ever expanded in a single year.

Suddenly Thomas Monaghan was a millionaire and he began to buy anything he wanted. In 1983 he bought the Detroit Tigers; one year later his team won the World Series. Monaghan purchased airplanes and about two hundred cars, including Deusenburgs, Rolls-Royces, and a 1929 Bugatti Royale which alone cost $8.1 million. He bought a north woods lodge located on 3,000 acres of land, complete with an airstrip, hangar, and a 580-foot pier on a lake (on which he floated a couple of yachts). This $30 million compound eventually boasted a championship golf course, bowling alley, and hotel.

Monaghan began to finance missions and mission projects in Honduras.

He enjoyed this so much he decided he would sell his company and do philanthropic work full-time. But by now the economy had soured, and he refused a couple of unacceptable offers.

Monaghan was so busy chasing multiple visions that he failed to notice he needed to seriously revise some of his company's business practices. His competitors did notice, however, and Pizza Hut and Little Caesar's quickly began to expand and take ever greater shares of the market. Domino's sales began to drop and some stores had to be closed.

What happened? In Monaghan's words, "I'd taken my eye off of the ball."

In the midst of the growing gloom, one night he was reading a book by C. S. Lewis titled, *Mere Christianity*. By the eighth chapter of this book, Monaghan recognized he was full of pride, the most deadly of all sins. He had spent years buying whatever he wanted, building a dream home, enjoying the high life. But this evening he remained sleepless. When morning came, he decided to stop building his house, to sell his cars, planes, and the resort. He would no longer do things just for show.

God had gotten Thomas Monaghan's attention. He testified that from then on, "I'd focus on God, family, and Domino's." Monaghan had realized that the very priorities that had gained him such huge success had been compromised by his own pride and distractedness. Courageously, he began to retrieve control of his destiny. He prioritized his life so that he could once again achieve long-lasting success.

Knowing his company was headed for disaster, he took the company off the market and immediately became its acting president. Unprofitable stores were sold and regional offices closed. After a year and a half of hard work and reinstituted priorities, Domino's was turned around by the man who had founded and still owned 97 percent of it.

In 1993, Domino's revenue hit $2.3 billion, with profits of at least $3 million a month. Its debt was cut in half, its stores all updated and computerized. Today Domino's operates stores in thirty-eight countries around the world.

Success. Almost disaster. Incredible success again. Why? Success came because a man fulfilled an entrepreneur's dream. Near disaster came when he allowed himself to be distracted by the rewards of success. Renewed success came because a man retrieved his original priorities. He began to focus on doing one thing well rather than being distracted by so many others.

In an interview with *Success Magazine*, Monaghan related his incredible story. His take on what he learned through it all:

> My life is less complicated now. I spend more time with my family. I don't watch T.V. I feel good about having gotten the distractions out of my system—maybe a little proud.[1]

Monaghan's struggle with priorities is the story of every American male and probably every male in the world. Who wouldn't like his life to be less complicated? Who wouldn't like to spend more time with his family? Who wouldn't like to stop being so distracted by everything?

I believe the key to all of these things is found in determining and maintaining right priorities. Each of us must determine the proper place of God, family, and business, just as Monaghan did.

A Spiritual Champion's Priorities

You have been called to be a spiritual champion. Spiritual champions are men of priority. They know who they are and what they are to do. They do not get distracted long-term. They are men of focus. Men of faith. Men of priority. Men of God. I'm convinced that men discover their meaning in life only when their priorities are right.

> Spiritual champions are men of priority. They know who they are and what they are to do. They do not get distracted long-term. They are men of focus.

As a pastor, I have the privilege of marrying many young couples who have determined that God wants them to spend the rest of their lives together. As these starry-eyed men and women meet with me, I quickly level with them about marriage. I tell them no one has ever come to my office for premarital counseling with the intention of getting a divorce. All of them come in with the greatest of intentions, but before long some of them see their dreams and even their lives shattered into a million pieces.

What's usually the problem? Priorities. I try to explain to each couple the importance of having the right priorities in life. I describe what I believe those priorities should be personally and as a married couple. I say that if mutual priorities are not adopted by each partner, disaster is just around the corner. Then I make a statement which shocks some people, but which I believe is incontestably true. I tell them, "A couple has a better chance of making it when they have shared priorities, *even if those priorities are wrong.*" Why is this so? Because if one partner has the right priorities and the other has the wrong ones, they can't even talk, let alone agree. Without shared priorities, a long-term relationship is threatened.

Right priorities are critically important in the life of a spiritual champion. If he is single, priorities are essential to help him remain pure and one day marry the "right" woman. If he is married, priorities are essential if he is to enjoy a meaningful and happy marriage. If he has children, priorities are essential in training up his children and grandchildren in the nurture and admonition of the Lord. Future generations are shaped by men with the right priorities in life.

Would you take a few moments to answer the following questions? Don't just read them through, but deal seriously with each of them. Meditate upon them before you continue reading this chapter.

Questions, Questions

- Is your life sometimes in disorder? If so, why?
- Why does disharmony come in relationships, even those within your own family?
- Do you ever become disgusted with the various tasks of life, especially those that disrupt plans and demand an alteration of what you want to do with your time? If so, why?
- Does indecisiveness occur within you or your family when a situation requires decision-making? If so, why?

The answer to each of the previous questions is related to your priorities. When a problem arises, either our priorities are wrong, non-existent, or we fail to live by what we say we believe.

Right priorities are as important to our lives as blood is to our body. Without blood we are dead. Without healthy blood we face major physical problems. With healthy blood, we can live a vital and productive life.

When our priorities are right we will enjoy a life of meaningful spirituality and personal fulfillment. When our priorities get out of line, we will face continuous struggles and problems until they are properly aligned. When proper priorities do not exist in our lives, spiritual life cannot exist, and we have absolutely zero direction.

Thinking through the following five areas has helped me to formulate a list of proper priorities. I believe they can do the same for you. Spend some time mulling over each of them, then develop your own list of priorities. If you are to reach the winner's circle as a spiritual champion, the priorities you choose (or perhaps reaffirm) are the vehicles that will send you there.

Personal Fellowship with God

The heart of America was captured on Friday, June 2, when Air Force Captain Scott O'Grady's F-16 was shot down by Bosnian Serbs. He lived through a pilot's worse nightmare. For six days he was hungry and hunted in a hostile land. The bountiful resources of the American military were appropriated to discover whether he was dead or alive. If alive, they were committed to his rescue.

Early on the morning of June 8, O'Grady made contact with a United States aircraft. Within five hours he was rescued and sitting on board the U.S.S. Kearsarge. When American television interviewed O'Grady, he always spoke of God. He was grateful to God alone for the miracle of keeping him safe through those six days. He spoke of prayer and how he talked with God continually. He knew his rescue was a miracle of God.

Time magazine recorded O'Grady's strong testimony of his prayers and commitment to God. O'Grady said,

> I prayed to God and asked Him for a lot of things, and He delivered throughout the entire time . . . .When I prayed for rain, He gave me

rain. One time I prayed, "Lord, let me at least have someone know I'm alive and maybe come rescue me." And guess what? That night T.O. [fellow F-16 pilot Thomas O. Hanford] came up on the radio.[2]

The rest is history. O'Grady was rescued, expressed his gratitude to Hanford, but most of all, he gave glory to God.

Men who are spiritual champions are careful to build and strengthen their fellowship with Jesus Christ. To them, this is above all else. O'Grady's relationship with God was the only thing that sustained him through his trials. And it will also be the only thing that sustains you.

> **Spiritual champions are are careful to build and strengthen their fellowship with Jesus Christ. To them, this is above all else.**

During the forty days I spent in prayer and fasting for revival in America, my church, and my life, the Lord continually impressed upon me that I was to commune with Him with my whole heart. In numerous passages in Psalm 119 God spoke to my heart about the importance of giving, serving, and communing with my whole heart to Him. Psalm 119:2 says, "How blessed are those who observe His testimonies, who seek Him with all their heart." Eight verses later it says, "With all my heart I have sought Thee; do not let me wander from Thy commandments." And Psalm 119:145 says, "I cried with all my heart; answer me, O LORD! I will observe Thy statutes."

In each of these verses (as well as others in this psalm) we discover the importance of coming to God with our whole heart. God does not desire part of us or a portion of our affections; He wants all of us.

Jesus affirmed this crucial principle. When speaking about the affairs of everyday life, the Master challenged His followers to seek Him first. Matthew 6:33 tells us, "But seek first His kingdom and His righteousness; and all these things shall be added to you."

The very reason Jesus Christ came to earth was to make it possible for us to have a relationship with Him. He wants to enjoy fellowship with us, not as one among many suitors, but as the Love of our lives. Jesus called for our allegiance to Him and to His kingdom first. This means above everything else.

The only way any of us can keep on winning as a spiritual champion is to place our personal relationships and fellowship with Jesus Christ as number one in our lives. Spiritual failure, family failure, and business failure will become a way of life if Christ is not number one. He is the only One who can keep a spiritual champion together, from beginning to end.

The Place of Family

A spiritual champion places his family as second in his life, second only to fellowship with Jesus Christ. What kind of signals are we giving to our families? Do they know where they stand on our priority lists? Or are the signals we're giving them telling them all the wrong things?

Ask yourself a few important questions about your family:

- Does my wife know she is the most important person in my life? How does she know?
- Do my children know they are the most important people in my life? How do they know?

Our families will know what kind of priority we are giving them only when we demonstrate, time and time again, our allegiance to keeping them at the highest place in our lives.

At times, we have to take extreme action to get things in order in this area of life. One of the most prominent men in contemporary American Christianity did just that in 1995. He walked away from one of the greatest coaching jobs in America, setting an example to hundreds of thousands of men across America who now look up to him as a spiritual champion. Most of all, he set an example for his family.

Sports Illustrated was stunned at his action, as was the entire sports world. *SI* titled its article about him, "Putting His House In Order." Bill McCartney left his coaching position at powerhouse Colorado University to bring needed healing to his family. Now *that's* a spiritual champion!

> **Our families don't want our wealth, our gifts, our prestige, or our applause. They want *us*.**

Men, it is past time that our families knew their place in our lives. It is time to take action, even extreme action if necessary. Our families don't want our wealth, our gifts, our prestige, or our applause. They want *us*. They want to know that, other than God, they are the most important thing in our lives.

Our marriage and raising our children is not some dress rehearsal. We have one shot at these two strategic privileges. Our wife's feelings should not be up for grabs. Our children's activities, from a piano recital to a ball game, are the most important agenda of our day after time with Jesus Christ. Don't kid yourself—they will remember if you were (or weren't) there. And don't forget that our model of what a true father should be will determine the future of our children's marriage and family life. Too much is at stake for us to allow our priorities to get out of order.

The Place of Church

Involvement with a local church ought to be third on our priority list, behind only our relationships with Christ and our families. Jesus died for the Church; He did not die for our business or job. He did not die for our golf game. He did not die for our civic club or booster club. He died for the Body.

The Church is not a building, the Church is a people—the people of

God. A church is where most people are introduced to God and where all people are to worship God. The Bible says in Hebrews 10:25, "Not forsaking our own assembling together, as is the habit of some, but encouraging one another, and all the more, as you see the day drawing near."

> **Jesus did not die for our business or job. He did not die for our golf game. He did not die for our civic club or booster club. He died for the Body.**

God has made it plain that the assembling of His people is very important in the life of a believer. It is vital to our spiritual life.

I know of some misguided who think church is only for old women and children. Of course, I don't know of any spiritual champions who display such an attitude. No one can live for God apart from the local church. God is calling you to help Him storm the gates of hell. He does not need wimps, but warriors. Fighting men. Godly men. Spiritual champions.

Anything great which God may be pleased to do in your life will be nurtured through a Bible-believing, teaching, and preaching church. The teaching of that church is essential to your spiritual health. It must teach the Word of God. Right doctrine is essential; we can't very well hit the target if we don't know where the target is. A Spirit-filled church will energize us to walk in holiness, to worship God with our whole hearts, and will teach us how to be men of God in our families.

Spiritual champions are spiritual leaders in their families and their churches. So go to work for God in your church. Be involved in ministry. Be disciplined and regular in your giving to your local church; don't defraud either yourself or your church of the privilege of giving of your best. Support fully your God-called pastor and, if he is accompanied by a staff, support them as well.

Now is the time for men to get serious about their relationships to Jesus' Church. You might even consider praying and fasting for spiritual revival to come to your church. If spiritual champions don't do it, who will? I'm convinced that the Church's spiritual condition throughout America will determine the future of our country. We are America's hope. And you can choose to be a part of what God will do.

The Place of Occupation

One of the greatest challenges men face today is in the American workplace. You don't need me to tell you that the pressure is great! Expectations are high. The trick is to balance the responsibility and necessity of work with the higher priorities of God, family, and church.

The Bible says that through honest work, men are to provide for themselves and their families. Never does Scripture hint that work ever takes the place of a personal relationship and fellowship with Jesus Christ. Never is work to take precedence over the family. Never is work to take us away from the worship of and service to God through our local churches.

Yet the temptation is strong to sacrifice our walks with Jesus, our families, or our churches on the altar of our jobs and careers. We must not forget that a job is merely a means to an end. It is the God-ordained means that supplies our needs. It is never to be the tail that wags the dog.

I think it's telling that the majority of men I meet today are not happy in their jobs. While some of them are mismatched in a career not meant for them, I wonder if a greater reason has to do with wrong priorities. How could a man be truly happy in a job if the three arenas of life which God has placed ahead of job—Jesus, family, church—have been "demoted"? If that man is a Christian, the answer is, he couldn't be. Even if he got true satisfaction out of his job, he will not be a happy man if the other three higher-priority items are somehow out of whack.

Spiritual champions understand the true place of work in their lives. They know that a job is the means God has given to them to meet their needs. It is where God has placed them to have an influence for Him. It also represents part of their contribution to society.

So whatever your job is, keep it in perspective. Don't let it run your life. Let it serve the purpose for which God intends for it in the life of a spiritual champion.

The Place of Recreation

Men love to play. And do you know what? God wants us to play! It renews us physically, emotionally, and spiritually. Recreation has a very special place in the life of a spiritual champion.

What we need most concerning play and recreation is perspective. Men are always prone to extremes. Balance should be the order of the day. While recreation is pivotal in a healthy spiritual champion—whether it be hunting, fishing, football, basketball, exercise, lawn care, civic club activity, or whatever helps recreate you—let's just remember to keep it in perspective!

Never should recreation precede the priorities of our personal relationships and fellowship with Jesus Christ. Never should it precede our families. Never should it precede our churches. Never should it precede our jobs. Recreation is important, but let's keep it in perspective. It should always be the final area of any man's priorities. If it is not, too quickly it becomes sin. Rather than recharging our batteries and getting us ready to join the fray once more, it can cause major stress in areas that eventually can bring great damage to our lives.

Right priorities. They can be a tall order, can't they? I admit that it's a lot simpler to write about priorities than it is to keep them in place! Yet all of us can do it, through Christ. Spiritual champions have been equipped to be conquerors in the most difficult areas of life.

I freely grant that the challenge of defining, adopting, and living by right priorities is a challenge bigger than you or I. But that's the Christian life; it's not for wimps, whiners, or weaklings. God will never ask us to live this lifestyle without equipping and enabling us to do so through His Spirit. Without question, living by these priorities requires Spirit-filled living. Yet they are the priorities of a spiritual champion.

> "The challenge of defining, adopting, and living by right priorities is a challenge bigger than you or I. But that's the Christian life; it's not for wimps, whiners, or weaklings."

How to Determine Your Priorities

On the day in 1995 that God brought a great spiritual revival to the congregation I pastor, men wept and repented when the Holy Spirit revealed to them that their priorities were not aligned with the Word of God. They were broken over unconfessed sin in their lives.

Spiritual champions need to know where and how to determine their priorities. This is essential to their spirituality and for their fulfillment as men. Two steps of action are required to determine proper priorities.

Let the Bible be your guide.

Throughout the Bible we learn the importance of God's Word in the life of a believer. The Bible provides direction, counsel, wisdom and correction for us. Psalm 119:105 says, "Thy word is a lamp to my feet, and a light to my path." The Word of God tells us how to walk the Christian life. It lights our path. The secret to living a life directed by right priorities is letting the Bible be our guide.

How do we discover God's priorities? By getting into His Word. It's wonderful to sit under the teaching of a godly, trained minister who can help us better understand the Bible, but that is no substitute for digging into the Word on our own. It's a well-known fact of learning that people gain the most when they discover a principle for themselves.

So get into the Word. Take the plunge. A godly man who has learned and is living by the principles of the Word of God is worth a dozen Ph.D.s who know Greek and Hebrew but who have little interest in walking with God.

Answer the hard questions of life.

Spiritual champions cannot ignore the hard questions of life. They must be answered. Often times those hard questions revolve around the areas of spirituality, family, church, job, and recreation.

- What place is your relationship and fellowship with God going to have in your life?
- What place is your family going to have in your life?
- What place is your church going to have in your life?
- What place is your job going to have in your life?
- What place is recreation going to have in your life?

If we will deal seriously with each of these questions from the Word of God, we will find the answers to the hard questions of life. I can't answer them for you, but by combining these two steps, you will be able to determine your priorities.

Results of a Rightly Prioritized Life

When a spiritual champion works through the Word of God and determines God's direction concerning his priorities, at least three results will appear in his life.

1. Order. When a spiritual champion gets his priorities aligned with the Word of God, he will enjoy order in his life. Confusion will cease. Order will reign.

If you want to exchange confusion for order, then discover the priorities of a spiritual champion. The process will bring order in an otherwise chaotic world.

2. Unity. The goal of a family is not union, but unity. You can tie the tails of two tomcats together and throw them over a fence and get union, but you won't have unity. The goal in a family is to enjoy unity. In fact, our entire lives will be graced with unity when our priorities are aligned with God's Word.

Unity is not only an attitude and atmosphere, but an experience. When we develop a spiritual champion's priorities, we will enjoy unity.

3. Decisiveness. Indecision causes problems in every area of life. When does indecision occur? When we do not know what to do or are uncertain about what should be done. Such indecision can afflict all areas of life.

When a spiritual champion determines God's priorities for his life, the groundwork which will shape all of his decisions already has been laid. When a decision must be made, he applies his pre-determined priorities to the situation. The result? Decisiveness—a natural consequence of a rightly prioritized life.

A Personal Word

When I first began in ministry, my goals were minimal. Growing up in a tiny church and living in a small town had capped my vision for anything greater. Due to God's sovereign grace, God opened doors for me to attend college and eventually seminary. Almost immediately my world grew bigger.

Before long, the Lord began to use me far beyond my own comprehension. His anointing was clear in the appearance of several ministry opportunities. Soon colleagues in the ministry began to talk to me about things I had never considered. One of these was ministry "success." I knew little about what they were describing, but soon I found myself being enticed toward the "bigger and better" in ministry, whatever that is.

In those moments of enticement toward the ladder of ministry "success," I became indecisive. I was faced with a choice. Would I go with God in His way and time, or would I yield to a false little god called "ministry success" that was begging me to become its next victim?

I realized this was really no choice at all. I returned to my priorities. I knew what God had called me to do and I wanted to do it with the purest of motivations. God enabled me to align my life with the priorities of God. I didn't have the discipline to live by these priorities, but God gave me the strength to do so.

When I allow the Holy Spirit to fill me daily, I am energized to fulfill these priorities. As one man who has worked through the process and who faces the daily challenge, just like you, I can tell you—it works!

I believe if God had not moved in my life to enable me to work through these issues, I would have lost all that is really important in life. Ministry success is important to me, but it's not worth sacrificing the higher priorities I've adopted from the Word of God.

A spiritual champion is a man who has developed, adopted, and who lives by godly and biblical priorities. When he consistently lives by these godly priorities, he learns the real meaning of a man. He fulfills God's destiny for his life. And a spiritual champion is always interested in that.

S T U D Y   Q U E S T I O N S

1. Has there ever been a time when you've "taken your eye off the ball," as Thomas Monaghan did? If so, explain.

2. If you had to name your top five priorities, what would they be, and in what order would you put them? How do these priorities translate into action in your life?

3. How did you answer the four questions on page XX [Questions, Questions]?

4. Read Matthew 6:33. Would you say that your life aligns pretty well with this verse, or not so well? Explain.

5. Where would you say that your family fits in your order of priorities? Do you think they would agree? Why or why not?

6. Read Hebrews 10:25. Where does church fit into your order of priorities? Do you think you've achieved a healthy balance here? Explain.

7. How many hours do you figure you spend at work in an average week? Does your wife or family begrudge any of this time? Explain.

8. What do you like to do for recreation? How much time do you suppose you spend on this activity in an average week? Do you believe this represents a good balance? Why or why not?

9. How is the Bible to be our guide? How does it guide our lives? Does it guide yours? Explain.

10. Which of the following results of living a prioritized life are evident in your life, and which do you wish you saw more of? Explain your answers:

A. Order

B. Unity

C. Decisiveness

CHAPTER SIX

The Influence of a Spiritual Champion

H e is one of the most influential men in America. He champions the causes of Christianity, family, and morality as much as any man alive today. His message strikes a responsive chord even in the ears of those who are non-Christians, but who are concerned about the direction America is heading. When he speaks, almost everyone listens.

Yet neither his appearance nor his personality are particularly charismatic. He does not tell horror stories of his past, how he was delivered from drugs, alcohol, or a bad marriage. Yet his influence is immeasurable.

He freely volunteers that his own dad had a tremendous influence on his life. He recalls how his dad spent three to four hours a day in prayer when he was conducting spiritual meetings. His godly mother raised him according to Christian morality and biblical teachings. Both parents helped shaped him into what he is today.

By all accounts, he considers himself quite ordinary. While his passion is obvious, his lack of pretense and his vulnerability are traits that draw people to him. What you see is what you get.

He is a trained psychologist, a noted academician, and a true authority on family life. Millions of readers buy his books and listen to him on his daily radio program. He can move the Christian community toward action as quickly and capably as anyone alive today, yet he is not a preacher or a politician.

No doubt you've already guessed that I'm talking about Dr. James Dobson. Without question, God has raised up this ordinary man to give an extraordinary message to America.

Dr. Dobson is the founder and leader of what may be the most influential ministry in America today. "Focus on the Family" can be heard all across America, while his many books are best sellers the moment they are released.

It's not hard to identify his heart: it is expressed throughout his books and broadcasts. He wants to see America come back to God, to return to Christian values. His heart longs for the family to be all God wants it to be. He and his wife, Shirley, desire to see a mighty spiritual awakening in America.

Dr. Dobson is not a politician, but a prophet. While he started out as a practicing psychologist, God had prepared him for more.

In Dr. Dobson, God found a man who was willing to stand alone. A man who was willing to pay the price, regardless of the cost. He was not looking for a position, or even the recognition of men; he was a man with a burden to call this nation back to Christian values and understanding.

This is why God has raised him up in our generation. God does not raise up men without convictions, but rather men who are willing to speak the truth. Dr. Dobson is one of those men. This is why his advice is sought by presidents and senators. This is why millions listen to him and read his books. God has raised him up to be a strategic leader who is helping shape the future of America.

In *Dr. Dobson: Turning Hearts Toward Home*, Rolf Zettersten closes his book with several of the principles which make James Dobson the influential spiritual champion he is. Zettersten mentions fourteen such principles, but I want to mention just three that stand out to me.

First, Dr. Dobson is a man with *a keen sense of the presence of God*. The Lord's presence lives in and through this spiritual champion. I have sensed it hundreds of times on his broadcasts. His honesty, vulnerability, humility, and brokenness are all signs that the presence of God impacts his life greatly.

Second, Dr. Dobson believes that *each of us must fight to preserve our values*. He champions this conviction as well as any leader in contemporary America. He knows the followers of Satan are playing for keeps. He also understands that each of us, especially men, must become involved in fighting to save our nation from the barbaric influences that have influenced us for the last forty years.

Third, Dr. Dobson is a man who understands that *life is short*. In a personal conversation with Zettersten, Dr. Dobson once stated,

> I would feel satisfied if I could achieve just three goals with my life. First, I want to stand before my Creator and hear the words: "Well done thou good and faithful servant. Enter into the joy of the Lord." Second, I want to take as many people as possible to heaven with me. Third, I want to see my parents again. I want Shirley to be there, and I want to spend eternity with my children.[1]

When speaking of the sudden death of the great basketball star, Pete Maravich, who died in his arms, Dr. Dobson gave this gripping reflection on the significance of Maravich's life and death:

> Yes, we say our purpose is to preserve families and make married

life more meaningful. That is true. But it is a secondary objective. Our primary reason for existence is to cooperate with the Holy Spirit in the salvation of every person we can possibly reach. Preserving families, you see, is our way of accomplishing that goal.[2]

You may not be as gifted or talented as Dr. James Dobson. Very few people are. But it's important that you understand God wants you to influence the future of this country. You may be as ordinary as Dr. Dobson, but God is able to do extraordinary things through your life.

> **God wants you to influence the future of this country. You may be ordinary, but God is able to do extraordinary things through your life.**

The most significant observation I have made in studying the life of Dr. James Dobson is that, through him, you can see what God can choose to do with just one man—just one man who would speak the truth to all people with great conviction and passion.

Leadership Is Influence

There exist multiple definitions of leadership, yet I always return to the one I believe is the most succinct of all: *leadership is influence*. Each man has influence. Each man is a leader; the only question is if he's a good leader or a poor one.

Few of us influence only one person. Most of us influence several people in this world. Others may influence hundreds or even thousands. A handful may influence countless thousands. The issue is not how many people we influence, but what kind of influence we have? Do we influence people for the cause of Christ? Do we influence them with our passion and conviction about major issues of life? When they are with us, do they know we are Christians who believe in Christian morality and that we want to see America enjoy a mighty spiritual awakening?

In other words, are we poor or great leaders to those around us?

Count on this. Whatever influence we have in life, God has given it to us. Therefore, we are to use it for Christ.

Spiritual champions use their influence for Jesus Christ. You won't find people yawning around them because of their lack of conviction. True spiritual champions influence people not only through their words, but by the strength of their convictions and by the decisiveness of their actions.

For too long we have allowed left-wing political activists to gain success in their anti-God, anti-family, and anti-morality agendas. Their barbaric influence has nearly eliminated the very mention of God from public schools and most public forums. Their warped morality has carved out an influential platform for the homosexual community. Their moral relativism has become the acceptable norm for most Americans, replacing the moral absolutes pre-

> **❝**
> Spiritual champions use their influence for Jesus Christ. You won't find people yawning around them because of their lack of conviction.
> **❞**

sented in God's Word. Much of modern day "Christianity" has been affected by liberalism to such a degree that the gospel is watered down and convenience is the message, rather than commitment.

Guys, we have been quiet for too long. It is time to use our influence for Jesus Christ. We need not be intimidated by the roar of a lion; the life of one godly man reduces the roar to nothing more than a hoarse meow. Spiritual champions are spiritual leaders. They influence the people they know for God, family, and morality. It is time for all of us to get off the sidelines and stop watching the James Dobsons of our day carry the ball by themselves. It will take each of us doing what we can if America is to come back to God.

The Marks of Influential Leadership

As we prepare to enter the twenty-first century, the hope for America is found in committed Christian men. One of the great men of the Bible reminds me of the kind of leaders we need in our contemporary culture. Where are the Nehemiahs in America?

Nehemiah is one of my favorite Old Testament characters. His book is one of my favorites. He was the kind of influential leader in his culture that we need today. If you read his book, you'll find that it contains many invaluable principles on effective leadership.

The only passage of Scripture from Nehemiah that I want to directly refer to in this chapter is found in 1:3-4.

> And they said to me, "The remnant there in the province who survived the captivity are in great distress and reproach, and the wall of Jerusalem is broken down and its gates are burned with fire."
> Now it came about when I heard these words, I sat down and wept and mourned for days; and I was fasting and praying before the God of heaven.

This passage is the motivation for everything that Nehemiah did for his city and country. Times were desperate, the future bleak. Nehemiah knew that God needed to be respected once again among His people in the city of Jerusalem.

From Nehemiah's life I want to point out ten marks of influential leadership. This is the kind of leadership that is needed to save our cities, our towns, our states, and our country. And it's needed *now*.

Burden

Nehemiah was a man with a burden. A burden is something you go to bed with, something you get up with, and something you live with daily. (No, I am not talking about your wife!) It consumes you in your thoughts, passions, and dreams. You dwell on it and fervently wish you could change it.

Nehemiah was so burdened with his devastated homeland that he fasted and prayed and wept and mourned for days on end. Finally he sought permission from the king to do something about it. He requested that he might rebuild its walls so that once again the people of God would enjoy dignity and security. He was sick and tired of Satan's crowd making God's people look powerless and His city look puny. He wanted to see the city restored to vitality, purpose, and life. Everything Nehemiah did began with a burden.

What is your burden? What keeps you awake at night? Is it the condition of the family? Is it the deadly tide of drugs that is sweeping this nation? Is it the disgrace of the growing numbers of homeless people crowding the streets of our great cities? What is it?

A burden isn't something you simply choose from a long list of possibilities. A burden strong enough to drive you to action comes only from God. Not everyone is called to get involved with the homeless, or with educational issues, or with the family. But every spiritual champion will be burdened with something. So I ask again: What's your burden?

If you don't know, then I recommend you spend some time with God. He has a burden just for you! He wants you to use your influence to deal with that burden. Ask God for a burden. As He supplies this burden to you, He will give you a vision. In fact, that vision will be enlarged. It will be God-size!

My own burden is for this great nation of ours.[3] This burden is often so great that it moves me to tears, a sense of mourning, meaningful prayer, and prolonged fasting. I simply can't ignore America's spiritual condition. I can't pass it off as if it were simply a television show. I know it is not. This is the greatest nation in the world, but it needs a great and mighty spiritual awakening. As America's spiritual condition goes, so goes the future of this nation. That's my burden. If you don't have one, why don't you ask God if it should be yours, too?

Vision

God gave Nehemiah a vision to rebuild the walls surrounding the city. He knew these rebuilt walls would once again bring security to the people and would be another step in returning the city to its former greatness. Jerusalem was to be the city of God.

What is vision? Vision is seeing something before it exists physically. Vision is a God-given ability to see some of what God sees. Nehemiah saw the city as strong and powerful even when its walls were weak and contemptible.

Our vision will never be any greater than our burden. Nehemiah's vision matched his burden. Yours will also. If you do not have a vision of God doing something great, it is because your burden is not great.

Tenacity

Nehemiah was a leader with great tenacity. In the face of fierce opposition—a common reaction against vision and leadership—Nehemiah held firm to his convictions and persevered to the end. The people who opposed his visionary leadership failed to stop him. This "cold water committee" was shown to be as toothless as the one who roars like a lion, namely Satan. In the face of godly, influential leadership, God's enemies are powerless.

Many leaders run when they hear the first whimper of negativism, but not Nehemiah. The Bible doesn't say so, but I think his middle name was Tenacity. He was tenacious for his vision, his faith, and despite opposition.

Many men are tenacious, but about the wrong things. They are tenacious about making money, becoming successful, doing their own thing, and playing with their grown-up toys. Christian men who are tenacious about worldly things are a major part of the problem in America. Men, we need to understand that we are part of the remnant of God.

> **How can the country get right with God if the remnant is off playing with tinker toys? As the remnant goes, so goes the nation.**

How can the country get right with God if the remnant is off playing with tinker toys? As the remnant goes, so goes the nation.

Spiritual champions are tenacious about the right things, as was Nehemiah. When the "anti" groups come out, they don't run away from them, but to them. In Christian love, they speak the truth. They are as tenacious for their vision as their opponents are for theirs. You can count on this: The one with the greatest tenacity will probably win the battle.

Facilitator

A facilitator is someone who helps a task move along by getting other people involved, according to their gifts and interests. Nehemiah was a facilitator. He got people involved, according to their giftedness, in accomplishing his God-given vision of rebuilding the wall around Jerusalem.

Real leadership always gets people involved in reaching their goals. When a leader facilitates the actions of others, he greatly enhances his effectiveness.

The influence of a spiritual champion is contagious. He gets people involved in turning others toward God, family, and morality. He knows he cannot do it alone. He shares his burden with others and gives them a way to be involved. He knows enough to educate them about how they can be personally involved.

Facilitating leadership is not a new concept. It is as old as Nehemiah. And it is what is needed today in order to see our nation come back to God, family, and morality.

Standard-Bearer

Opposition always surfaces against godly leadership. If the leader or the people who follow him focus their attention on the voices of opposition, discouragement is inevitable. God's people did just this, but not Nehemiah the leader. In the midst of opposition he lifted up the standard. He called his people back to God and reminded them why they were doing what they were doing. When he was through, the people no longer wanted to quit, but were filled with a new enthusiasm to continue.

In our desire to make a difference we must always remember to lift the standard high. The standard is not ours, but God's. Evil situations will only turn around to the degree that leaders are willing to lift the standard.

Negotiation may be a given in business, but not in morality. We cannot sacrifice the place of God, family, and morality on the altar of negotiation or compromise. Spiritual champions are standard-bearers. God's standard must be held high in our families, communities, schools, churches, and our personal lives.

Strategist

Nehemiah was a strategic leader. He had a plan for the people. He prepared them for every kind of situation and created an attitude of cooperation, victory, and perseverance. His strategic leadership is one of the major reasons the people of God completed the project in the teeth of intense opposition.

Spiritual champions must be strategic leaders wherever God had placed them. If their influence is to be felt, they must plan for it to happen. What are you doing to make a difference in your world? What is your plan? How does God want to use you? Influential leaders are strategic leaders.

Motivator

In the midst of deep discouragement, Nehemiah became an exceptional motivator. By focusing the people on completing the wall, he kept them motivated to accomplish the work. When they considered quitting, he provided the nudge which inspired them to continue.

People are motivated when we cast a clear vision before them by encouraging them, calling them to excellence, and reminding them that fulfillment is found only in Jesus Christ. As Nehemiah motivated the people in this manner, they completed the task.

We need leaders who can motivate people to positive and godly change. Inconsistent leadership does not motivate. Whether it is in our home, relationships, business, or community, we must always remember that as the leader goes, so go the people. Leadership is influence. As the people go, so goes the project.

Whatever it is that you are trying to get people to accomplish, they will only succeed to the degree to which they remain motivated. It's your job as a spiritual champion to provide that nudge of encouragement.

Follow-Through

Nehemiah's burden determined his vision. As he got the people involved, his tenacious leadership provided the needed motivation to complete the project. In fifty-two days—less than two months—the wall was rebuilt around Jerusalem. Nehemiah's life, vision, and words were authenticated by the completion of the wall. As always, follow-through demonstrates the leader's integrity.

As a pastor, I have led people since 1976. I'm convinced one of the distinguishing marks of leadership is follow-through. Influential leaders complete projects. They follow through on what they say.

As spiritual champions, we must be men who keep our promises and who complete our projects. Our leadership and integrity are put in jeopardy the moment we fail to follow through on what we began.

Influential leaders not only start well, but finish well. Nothing is more discouraging or frustrating than attempting to follow someone who does not follow through. Trust diminishes when people do not deliver on what they say they are going to do. And no spiritual champion can afford a breakdown in trust.

Bible-Centered

Nehemiah was a Bible-centered leader. He called people to a commitment to God's Word. He urged them to let God's Word be their authority.

Spiritual champions will always uplift and embrace the Bible as the Word of God. It is the only manual that determines their direction.

People are looking for definitive leadership. We can provide this kind of leadership only as we point people to the Word of God. Bible-centered leadership results in spiritual renewal among the people. Any time people obey God's Word, spiritual renewal is the natural result.

Celebrators

Nehemiah was a unique leader in many ways. Not many leaders would know how to lead the people in celebrating the victory of completing the wall—yet Nehemiah did. The people were filled with happiness, gladness, joy, excitement, singing, and praise. The more musical among them joined in with loud orchestral accompaniment.

Influential leaders remind people of their victories which were accomplished through Jesus Christ and His power. Whenever we influence people to make a difference in some area, we should celebrate with them when progress is made. Influential leaders do not simply run from one completed project to another; they spend time celebrating the victories.

How You Can Influence Your World

Nehemiah was just one man, but he determined many future generations of Jerusalem. His leadership made a major difference in the people of God.

You are not Nehemiah. You are not James Dobson. You are just you. But your gift mix was orchestrated by your Creator, and He desires for you to use your influence in whatever arena He's placed you. He wants you to be a man with . . .

A Holy Standard

Spiritual champions lift up the standard of God. In a day of amorality, we need to provide definitive leadership by declaring unashamedly the absolutes of God. God is unchanging. What was holy in Bible days is holy today. God's holiness is the standard that needs to be lifted up.

You and I are called to lift up this standard. It is to be our standard. We must lift up the standards of God to others. Our children and grandchildren need to view us as holy men of God. And they will if we will live by God's standard and call them to live by it as well! This is one of the major roles of influential leadership.

I wonder: Where are the men today who will lift up God's standard? Where are the pastors and church leaders who will lift up God's standard? Where are the politicians who will lift up God's standard? Where are the husbands and fathers who will lift up God's standard?

If you decide to answer the call, then be willing to pay the price. Jesus did. He set His face like flint to accomplish the task God gave Him, and He paid with His life. Yet He changed the world. He changed me. And He changed you.

Influential leaders are Jesus men. They mimic their leader. These spiritual champions sense they are destined to be men who lift up the standard of God.

God wants you to do something. I cannot determine what that is for you, but I pray He will give you a plan for influencing your own world. *Do something.* You can make a difference in the lives of those around you. God has a plan for you. Now your job is to determine what that plan is and do it!

Meaning and Influence

The real meaning of a man is discovered in being an influential leader. You have influence. What are you doing with it?

God can do more through you in a moment than you could ever do on your own in a lifetime. Those around you need to see in you and hear from you about your God. Wherever His presence is, things, places, people, and nations change. They are never the same again.

> God can do more through you in a moment than you could ever do on your own in a lifetime.

As you discover your destiny as a spiritual champion, you will see more and more places where you can be an influential leader. Those around you will begin to embrace God, family, and morality once again.

This is the work of real men. Influential leaders. Spiritual men. Spiritual champions.

S T U D Y   Q U E S T I O N S

1. Is it easy or difficult for you to stand alone? Explain. Describe a time when you did, or when you wished you had.

2. How does someone "sense" the presence of God? Do you think you have a keen sense of His presence? Why or why not?

3. What values do you hold that you would fight for? Why these particular values? What would you be willing to do to protect them? What have you done to protect them?

4. Read James 4:14. What reminder does this verse give us? How should this reminder affect the way we live? Does it in your case? Explain.

5. Who most influenced you? How did they do so?

6. Who is in your sphere of influence? How do you think you are you influencing them?

7. What burden, if any, do you take to bed every night? How does this burden shape your priorities and actions?

8. Do you have a vision of what God wants to do through you? If so, describe it. If not, would you like to have one? What do you think it would take to get one?

9. Do you consider yourself a tenacious person? Explain.

10. Discuss each of the following aspects of a good leader. Why is each important, and how well do you think you measure up in each area?

A. Facilitator

B. Standard-bearer

C. Strategist

D. Motivator

E. Follow-through

F. Bible-centered

G. Celebrators

11. Are you lifting up a "holy standard"? If so, what is it? If not, why not?

CHAPTER SEVEN

A Spiritual Champion's Sphere of Influence

Just before my sixteenth birthday, Jesus Christ changed my life. While I had attended church all my life and was raised in a Christian home, it wasn't until this experience that Jesus became my Lord and Savior. He touched me and began a mighty work in me, and in the winter of 1972 the Lord's calling became apparent. The next March I surrendered my life to preach the gospel of Jesus Christ.

That's when I started to run.

Oh, I wasn't running away from His calling or from His will. I was running as fast as I could to accomplish what I felt God wanted me to do. The Lord had so transformed me in salvation and His calling was so real that I was filled with boundless enthusiasm. Unfortunately, wisdom often lagged behind my zeal. Not infrequently I lurched ahead of God.

While at seminary, for example, I carried a full academic load while holding down a full-time pastorate. My poor wife sometimes didn't know if I was coming or going (and to tell the truth, neither did I).

But I was running!

Just as I began work on my doctoral degree, our first son, Josh, was born. And as the church grew, so did the demands of ministry. What could I do?

I kept on running.

After seminary, the church took over my life. I was living out the dreams God had given me while sitting in those seminary classrooms. I was having the time of my life. Meanwhile, our second son, Nicholas, was born. And on I ran.

My wife was understanding, but weariness began to overtake her (that will happen when you try to meet the needs of a busy husband and two active preschoolers). I was so grateful for her Herculean efforts, do you know what I did to help her?

I kept on running.

Of course, there were the late-night conversations any happy couple has. Just before you go to sleep, you notice her tone of voice and realize that you really ought to listen. So you try. Sometimes you discover you have to try listening almost the entire night. Sure, the conversation is a bit confrontational, but you think *She's just tired. She'll get over it.*

It's not that I didn't care. I did. It's just that I was busy. I was called to God's work! People had needs and I wanted to meet those needs! I had responsibilities, dreams, and goals! No person or thing was going to stop me from fulfilling them.

So I continued to run.

You know, there is Someone who knows how to stop an addicted runner. If He must, He will outrun you and be at the finish line before you arrive. If He has to, He will stop you dead in your tracks. If necessary, He will bring Holy Spirit conviction upon you to such a marked degree that you will discover, quite uncomfortably, that there's a lot more to repentance than what you learned in seminary textbooks.

Can you see where this is going?

In 1985, God made it clear that He wanted me to stop running. He wanted me to retire my Nikes and take a day off. Until then I had always interpreted this as weakness. I was a workaholic and proud of it. I could not stand being around lazy men, especially lazy preachers. But in that year, events transpired which convinced me that my family needed more of my time and attention.

Jeana was now the mother of two preschoolers and found herself dealing with stress levels exceeding the limit. She craved my understanding, my attention, and any free hand that I could offer.

Meanwhile, the church I pastored was increasing numerically—and suffering the turmoil of rapid growth. Such growth demanded appropriate transition, and it was clear that not everyone was willing to make the needed changes. Pressure mounted on every front.

Suddenly I was confronted by two pressure points. My wife needed me while my church demanded everything from me. Since the birth of my first son, I knew adjustments needed to be made, but . . . Now, after five years of running from parental responsibilities, at last I realized that while churches come and go, my family would always be with me. Therefore, I had better get to know them and once more become an intimate part of their lives.

Sure, the church was growing and everyone around me considered me a success, but I knew the time had come to stop running. It was time to become the man God wanted me to be in my family.

I believe one reason God convicted me about my extreme work ethic was that He knew what lay ahead. He was getting me ready for the responsibilities I have today. He knew that if I did not get things in order and become the father and husband He wanted me to be, His work through my life would be limited.

I responded to the conviction of the Spirit and began to take some time off weekly. I became more understanding with my wife. I began to take extra time to be with my two boys. Do you know what? I fell in love with it! Today there is nothing more important to me than being with Jeana, Josh, and Nick.

The members of my congregation, whom I feared would criticize me for taking time off, instead loved and applauded me for doing so. I found they appreciated having a pastor who modeled family life to them.

In my drive to make a difference for Jesus Christ, I had spent years running ineffectively. My mistake was that I forgot the other spheres in my life, especially my family and friends. I needed balance in my life.

The Lord does want us to make a difference for Him around the world, but He wants us to begin in our own families. God has called all of us to be "difference-makers," but especially within certain appropriate spheres.

The Key Is Balance

Neither God nor His work should ever be put on the sideline, but keeping balance in our lives is crucial. Men learn their true meaning when they live a balanced life.

I believe the major reason that career so often dominates over family and money overshadows the will of God is that men are not living the Spirit-controlled life. When I feel compelled to "make it" in my career, I am striving in the flesh. God does not want His children living in the flesh; He does not want them living according to carnal principles. God wants them to live in the Spirit, which means according to spiritual principles.

> I believe the major reason that career so often dominates over family and money overshadows the will of God is that men are not living the Spirit-controlled life.

The balance is not between the Spirit and the flesh. The flesh life is wrong, unspiritual, and carnal. The balance occurs only as we are filled and controlled by the Holy Spirit. As God fills and controls us, He will enable us to maintain a balance dictated by godly priorities—the things that really matter in life.

If you feel as if you are spinning on a merry-go-round, then it's likely you are not being filled with the Spirit. God does not cause confusion, but brings order. God infuses wisdom into our lives which enables us to find balance in all the demands on us. The Holy Spirit is the key to this balance.

Our Relationship to the Holy Spirit

The spheres of influence in the life of a spiritual champion will depend on his relationship to the Holy Spirit. A spiritual champion under the control of the Holy Spirit will enjoy order and balance in his life. He will understand that the spheres of his influence are like concentric circles. As he is being filled with the Spirit, his influence will flow immediately to his family, then to his church, then to his friends, and then to other areas of life. These circles of influence will not be exchanged one for another depending on personal preferences, but will flow out normally as he moves from one circle to another, making a difference for Jesus Christ wherever he goes.

The Bible speaks often about the Holy Spirit. One of the monumental passages concerning our relationship to the Spirit is found in Ephesians 5:18. It says: "And do not get drunk with wine, for that is dissipation, but be filled with the Spirit."

Even as a drunk is under the control of wine, Christians are to be intoxicated and under the control of the Holy Spirit. It is God's will for us to be filled with and to be controlled by the Holy Spirit.

Once a man is changed by the grace of God at his spiritual conversion, the Holy Spirit comes into his life. At that moment the Spirit baptizes him into the family of God. The Spirit also endows him with various spiritual gifts and enables him to live the Christian life. The Holy Spirit wants to fill us daily, perpetually, moment-by-moment. He anoints men to fulfill the special assignments God gives to them.

We all need this kind of relationship with the Holy Spirit. This is God's will for us all. As we walk in His will, He will take us through the various spheres of our lives, under the control of His Spirit. That naturally brings up another question. What are the various spheres of influence in which God wants to use us? And how does He want us to be energized in them?

A Spirit-Controlled Leader in the Family

The most important person to model spirituality in our families is us. Spiritual leadership in the family is not to be delegated to our wives or to a spiritually maturing child. We will not discover our meaning as a man until we live the Spirit-controlled life.

One of the most frequently asked questions of me as a pastor regards male leadership in the family. "How can a man be the spiritual leader of his family?" While there are many answers, let's look at three of them. You can be the spiritual leader in your family by . . .

1. Modeling the Spirit-Controlled Life

The most important thing any of us can do for our families is to be filled and controlled by the Holy Spirit. Nothing we do will have a greater impact on our families than this. If we are not being filled with the Spirit, we are opening the front door of our home to Satan and saying to him, "Come on in." It is as important for the leader of the family to be filled with the Spirit as it is for the pastor of the church to be filled with

> If we are not being filled with the Spirit, we are opening the front door of our home to Satan and saying to him, "Come on in."

the Spirit. With the Spirit, there is leadership and unity; without the Spirit, there is chaos and confusion.

The sad truth is that many women today have to watch a television pastor or read Christian books in order to receive any spiritual leadership in their homes. Their husbands are not modeling the Spirit-controlled life, either to them or to their children.

The eternal and daily spiritual destiny of our families depends on us. Spiritual champions understand that their first role in the family is to model the Spirit-controlled life. This is far more important than providing materially. The will of God for us is to be filled with the Spirit. It is sin to not be filled with the Spirit.

2. Loving Your Wife

According to the apostle Paul, the major responsibility of a husband toward his wife—other than modeling the Christian life to her—is to love her. The Bible says in Ephesians 5:25, "Husbands, love your wives, just as Christ also loved the church and gave Himself up for her."

It has been said that the best thing a man can do for his children is to love their mother. For the most part, that's absolutely true. Loving your wife teaches your son how to relate to his future spouse. It shows your daughter what to expect from a godly husband. It gives breath and life to one of the most important lessons in life—a lesson which will affect your children, grandchildren, and great-grandchildren.

Paul says we are to love our wives with the same kind of love Jesus demonstrated toward His Church. And what kind of love was that?

Jesus loved the Church sacrificially, voluntarily, and unconditionally. You are to love your wife sacrificially by being willing to die for her, voluntarily by wanting to meet her every need, and unconditionally by accepting her at all times.

Do you realize how special your wife is? Have you ever tried to grasp her great value? Better yet—does she know what you think about these things? To love her is to show her how valuable she is to you.

Our only hope for loving our wives in this way is to be filled with the Spirit. By nature, most of us are egotistical beings. We always want *our* needs met. But what about the needs of our wives? There is no way we will ever get outside our self- interest to love her, unless we are being filled with the Spirit. This is our only hope to love her the way Jesus loves the Church.

It's been said many times before, but it bears repeating: The greatest thing we can do for our children is to love our wives like this. Nothing will gain their respect more than showing her Christ-like love. To love in this way will show our sons how to love their future wife and it will picture for our daughters how they should expect to be loved.

You can be the spiritual leader in your family by being controlled by the Holy Spirit and modeling the spiritual life before them. You can also be the spiritual leader in your family by loving your wife. But there is also another way you can be the spiritual leader in your family.

3. Discipling Your Children

Every father is instructed to disciple his children in the Christian faith. I do this through what I call "life lessons." Even though our family attempts to pray together daily, I do not set up a blackboard, get out my Bible, and teach an exposition of Scripture. I teach my boys the Word of God through real-life situations.

When something occurs that may be wonderful or tragic, blessed or sinful, I take three to five minutes to give my boys a "life lesson." Through applying the Word of God in this way, I am trying to teach them not only a spiritual principle, but that the Word of God is the most relevant book in the world.

Our children need to be accountable to us in their spiritual lives. Have we taught them the importance of reading the Bible daily? Have we taught them how to pray? Have we taught them the importance of a daily quiet time? Have we taught them how to share Christ and the importance of taking the gospel to the entire world? If not, where do we expect them to learn it?

As we teach our children these things, we must hold them accountable. Periodically ask them how they are doing in their spiritual lives. Listen when they talk to you. Discover where they are in their walk with Christ. Fathers cannot walk away from the God-given responsibility of nurturing their children in the ways of God.

> A good test of our spiritual walk with Christ is to evaluate our commitment to being the spiritual leader of our family.

As a spiritual champion lives under the intoxication or control of the Holy Spirit, he will wholeheartedly embrace being the spiritual leader of his family. A good test of our spiritual walk with Christ is to evaluate our commitment to this responsibility.

Spirit-Controlled Leader in the Church

The Church of Jesus Christ is to be led by godly, Spirit-filled men who are walking with Jesus Christ. When men are filled with the Spirit they are teachable. They want to learn about walking with Jesus Christ. They want to learn how to go on with God. They want to know what it really means to be a man.

One of the ways a man can demonstrate his teachability to the Lord is by making sure his family is in worship every week. I tell people the reason God called me to preach was that He knew I needed to be in worship almost daily. Listen—nothing is more important than bringing the family to experience the joy and privilege of worshipping the Living God.

A subtle movement today implies that we have to save the family from too much church. I have a great Arkansas word for that concept: Hogwash! Our families need to be under the Word of God continually. The first-century church was under God's Word daily in worship. Our culture today is doing all it can to choke the life of God out of our families. Our families need to be learning God's Word daily and worshipping together weekly.

When we take seriously our spiritual leadership role in the family, we will also take it in the church. We will serve the Lord with all of our hearts. We will not just "get by" or "get fed," but will desire to serve others in Jesus' name.

Spirit-controlled men are also supportive men of God in the church. They will not be "nay-sayers." They will be men who support a Spirit-controlled church, with a Spirit-controlled pastor, who is leading in a Spirit-controlled direction, taking the gospel to the world. If your church is not this kind of church, help it to become one. If it cannot, find one that can. Spiritual champions are not interested in convenience, but in a commitment to take the gospel of Jesus Christ to the world. This is the ultimate goal of a Spirit-filled man who is a part of a Spirit-filled church.

Spirit-Controlled Leader in the Workplace

A Spirit-filled man will have great spiritual influence on his job and in the workplace. He wouldn't think of embarrassing his Lord through a poor attitude, ungodly actions, or a sloppy, slothful work ethic.

A spiritual champion models real Christianity to people in the workplace. He consistently strives after a "4:13," "can do" attitude. He remembers that he is called to an "8:37," to "conquering actions." He responds to conflict in a spiritual manner. He knows that God has led him to that particular workplace in order to share his faith in Jesus Christ and make a difference for Him.

A Spirit-controlled man models a Christian work ethic. Slothfulness is not in his vocabulary. His life is filled with productivity and teamwork. His desire is for the good of all in the workplace, not just for himself.

When we model real Christianity and a godly work ethic in the workplace, we will be spiritual leaders. But these things are possible only as each of us is controlled by the Holy Spirit.

Spirit-Controlled Relationships

Disrupted and broken relationships represent a major hindrance to a mighty spiritual awakening in America. Relationships are broken when the parties involved are not being filled with the Holy Spirit.

Men need other men. Iron sharpens iron. Our relationships must become deeper than "buddies" in a hobby or in some form of recreation. Spiritual relationships with other men are crucial. All of us need friends. The best friendships are spiritually driven, resulting in harmony and love. God wants us to be Spirit-controlled, influential leaders in all of our relationships.

So far in this chapter I have described the importance of the Spirit-controlled life. Now I want to close the chapter with some of the most important truths you will find anywhere in this book. If we desire to live as spiritual champions, we must live the Spirit-controlled life. If we choose the carnal life over the Spirit-controlled life, we will forfeit the promises of God that belong to us. There's no reason to do that! Let's choose to be filled with the Holy Spirit. Our lives come into harmony when the Holy Spirit of God has the liberty to flow through us, influencing our whole being and life.

How to Be Controlled by the Holy Spirit

The Holy Spirit of God wants to control us. He wants to influence everything in our lives. Nothing in our lives will go untouched when we are being intoxicated and controlled by the Holy Spirit.

While I do not believe in most of the trite spiritual formulas that are being propagated today, in order to better understand this relationship with the Spirit, permit me to outline three necessary steps if we are to receive the filling of the Holy Spirit.

Step #1: Repentance of Sin

Repentance begins at salvation and does not end in this life. Continual repentance is the only way to maintain a mighty work of God. The word "repentance" means to have a change of mind and a change of direction. Repentance of sin is essential to our being filled with the Holy Spirit.

Even though every Christian is forgiven, we still sin. We must deal with that sin. A life of sin makes a deep walk with Christ impossible. Sin steals the intimacy from the relationship. Repentance maintains the closeness of our relationship with Christ. It breeds sweet fellowship with the Spirit.

> **Spiritual champions must deal with their sin. They must take it seriously, turn from it, and receive the freedom Christ has given them from it.**

Those who want to claim their destiny as spiritual champions must deal with their sin. They must take it seriously, turn from it, and receive the freedom Christ has given them from it. Spiritual champions desire to so live by the power of the Spirit that the need for repentance grows less and less because the hold sin has on them grows less and less. But when it is required, they do not shrink from it. They know that repentance is the quickest and only route back to full fellowship with their incomparable Lord.

As often as it is required, deal with your sin. Confess it to God. Claim the forgiveness God has freely given to you. Tell God you are turning from that sin and receiving the power to be freed from it. Then we can be sure that "He is faithful and righteous to forgive us our sins and to cleanse us from all unrighteousness" (1 John 1:9).

Step #2: Surrender Your Life

After we have dealt with our sin, we must surrender our lives to Jesus Christ daily. We must take this as seriously as we do turning from sin.

If we desire the Spirit's control in our lives, the second step is to surrender our whole being to Him—mind, body, emotions, will, everything. I believe it is also important to surrender our future, our past, and our present to Him, as well as our gifts, talents, and resources. Of course, it all belongs to Him anyway. Our acknowledgment that these things belong to Him is an act of surrender to the Spirit's leadership.

Step #3: Live by Faith

Being filled with the Spirit is not always an emotional experience. In fact, it probably will not be. Being filled or controlled by the Spirit is an act of faith. It is a lifestyle of faith. As we pray for the filling of the Spirit, we do so by faith.

Prayer is essential to being filled with the Spirit. As we follow these steps to be controlled by the Spirit, we do so in prayer. Allow me to give an example of how I ask to be filled with the Holy Spirit. I pray something like this:

"Dear Lord Jesus, I know I have sinned against you. I confess that _____ is sin. I turn from this sin and receive your freedom from it. I surrender my mind, the way I think. My will and what I want to do. My emotions and the way I feel. My body, all that I am. The members of my body I surrender to you—my eyes, ears, tongue, nose, arms, legs, hands, feet, sexual organs, and the rest of me. I am yours. I surrender to you. I want to be controlled by your Spirit. So, right now, in simple faith, I receive the filling of the Holy Spirit. Thank you for filling me, controlling me, and giving me spiritual victory."

Men, it is time we practice being filled with the Holy Spirit daily. When we are being filled with the Spirit, every sphere of our lives will be affected. Not one realm or sphere of life will go untouched. The Spirit will influence us and our lives in a supernatural way.

Let me urge you to ask God to fill you right now. If there is some sin that needs to be acknowledged and repented of, then do that immediately. Why delay? The blessing of the Spirit's filling is glorious; there's no reason to live without it.

So don't!

S T U D Y   Q U E S T I O N S

1. Why is "balance" such a key to life? Why is achieving balance often so difficult? What areas of life do you think you balance well? In what areas do you struggle to find balance?

2. What do you know about the Holy Spirit? Is He at work in your life? How can you tell?

3. Read Ephesians 5:18. What does it mean to be filled with the Spirit? How can you tell if this is happening in your life?

4. Who in your life has best modeled the Spirit-controlled life to you? What was so effective about their modeling?

5. Read Ephesians 5:25. What does loving your wife have to do with spirituality?

6. What does it mean to disciple your children? What kind of activities might this involve? Do you think you are discipling your own children? Explain.

7. What do your children learn about the importance of church based on your own involvement there?

8. How can you demonstrate Spirit-controlled leadership at work? What makes this difficult? How can you strive to overcome these difficulties?

9. Do you maintain significant friendships with other men that help keep you on track spiritually? If so, what do you do to maintain them? If not, why not?

10. Ronnie mentions three keys to living a Spirit-controlled life. Describe each of them and tell how they are worked out in your own life:

A. Repentance of sin

B. Surrender your life

C. Live by faith

CHAPTER EIGHT

What Spiritual Champions Need Most

The Olympic spirit is racing across this nation. The city of Atlanta, Georgia, is gearing up to host the 1996 Summer Olympic games. Another spark of Olympia was ignited recently when the people of Salt Lake City, Utah, learned they had been selected to host the 2002 Winter Olympics. America loves to associate with champions.

Behind the Olympic preparations and the lighting of the torch, the Olympic games are about world-class athletes competing against each another. Already they are champions in their own countries, but they dream of becoming world champions. Most of them have trained their entire lives to compete in the Olympics.

Olympic competition captures the attention of the world. Whether you are a lover of sports or not, Olympic fever is contagious. Teenagers, young adults, and even middle-aged adults with no prior name recognition can become international celebrities in a heartbeat.

Yet it's not merely great athletic skill that captivates our attention. Something more draws us into these Olympics every four years. What is it? I believe it is the inner qualities that enable these athletes to rise to championship status.

The Reader's Digest recently reprinted an article titled, "What Makes Olympic Champions?"[1] The author listed seven characteristics of an Olympic champion which result in success wherever they are applied.

Seven Characteristics

1. They have a dream. Most Olympic champions visualize themselves competing in the games even from childhood. They usually envision victory before they experience it.

2. They are fired up. A flame of competition burning inside seems common to all Olympic champions. The following words are worthy of note:

"The Olympic flame that top performers pursue burns inside them. They're driven not only to be the best but to do their best—always."[2]

This inner flame is what keeps the likes of Carl Lewis coming back for more. Even though Lewis holds eight gold medals, at age 36 he wants to compete again in the 1996 games in Atlanta. Olympic champions are driven by an inner flame that never goes out.

3. *They bounce back.* The media highlights those who win and a few who suffer great disappointment. Yet most of these Olympic athletes end up as losers in their chosen competition. For example, in the 1992 men's giant slalom, 133 men competed for the championship. Only three of these received medals. Yet it's often this very loss that inspires the other 130 to bounce back again in world-class competition.

4. *They aim high.* One of the greatest female athletes of all time is Florence Griffith-Joyner, better known as "Flo Jo." Prior to competing in the 1988 Olympic games she wrote in her diary the outcome and the time she expected to run in the 100-meter dash. She accomplished both. She wrote that she would win the 100-meter dash in a time of 10.54 seconds. When she crossed the finish line as champion, she had called her winning time to the split second. She aimed high and reached it. Amazing!

5. *They plan for trouble.* It is usually imperceptible to the untrained eye, but these champions improvise continually during a performance. If they miss a jump, they make an immediate adjustment. Even though hundreds of hours go into training and practice, in the heat of competition, plans are usually adjusted. A true Olympic champion anticipates these setbacks and prepares for them.

6. *They never quit.* Perseverance characterizes all athletes, especially world-class Olympians. They know they must complete their tasks regardless of the odds. The Olympic games have been filled with moments of tears, silence, and great applause for athletes who have fallen but who have then literally crawled for yards to cross the finish line.

7. *They make their own luck.* If the dark horse athlete is prepared and the favored athlete fails, a virtual unknown can become an instant celebrity. This is called, "making your own luck." It is being prepared for a big break in the midst of competition.

As these seven characteristics show, there is much more behind an Olympic champion than making the shot, finishing the jump, or getting the break. It goes above and beyond a stellar performance. These inner qualities are the driving force that result in world-class championships.

In the Heat of Competition

> A man can face no more intense competition in our godless culture today than living the Christian life.

A man can face no more intense competition in our godless culture today than living the Christian life. The American culture is hostile to the godly man. A real spiritual champion will almost certainly become the target of ridicule, jokes, and even persecution. The cost may be greater than we might imagine.

Yet being in the heat of this spiritual competition need not make us timid. Instead, we should allow it to spur us on to a holy boldness like that found in the life of the ultimate spiritual champion, Jesus Christ.

In case anyone is unaware of it, there's a war going on out there. The enemy is out to destroy us. He wants to shatter our marriages, ruin our kids, strip us financially, attack us physically, corrupt us mentally, and twist us emotionally. In other words, he wants to bring us down!

Who is this enemy? If you can stick him with a pin and he bleeds, he is not your enemy. Men, we are not in hand-to-hand combat with people. Let's not allow the enemy to confuse the issues or disguise his identity. Satan is our enemy. Our enemy is not a board of men, it is not our wives or children, it is not any of our colleagues. Our enemy is Satan.

In the heat of competition with this sly, cunning, powerful foe, we must stand tall as a spiritual champion. We are in a war—real, live, spiritual battle every day. Satan and his minions are attempting to intimidate men everywhere.

Well, I am sick of it. I refuse to retreat like a coward avoiding the battle. I want to be a warrior in the heat of the fight. I want my inner flame to burn brighter than all the flames of hell. I want to storm the gates of hell, rattling them and demanding that the captives be set free.

> **"** I want to be a warrior in the heat of the fight. I want to storm the gates of hell, rattling them and demanding that the captives be set free. **"**

We are men on a mission. Just as Olympic athletes are champions in the heat of competition, we must be spiritual champions. Our mission is to make a difference for Jesus Christ in this world. Whoever our life touches, we are to make an impact. Just like Jesus. He always made a difference wherever He went.

The competition Jesus faced was infinitely more intense than that of an Olympic athlete. The rivalry, criticism, and warfare He faced daily was greater than anything we will ever know. Yet though the pain, the struggle, and the ferocity of warfare we will face will never match the levels that confronted Jesus, we will face intense opposition. It's part of being a man, especially a spiritual champion.

Olympic champions know there is much behind the glitz and glitter that accompanies a big win. There is pain. Sacrifice. Early morning practice. Continual competition. Little rest. Constant training. Endless sacrifice.

In the same way, there is another side of the Christian life which some of us may know little about. The Christian life is more than just streets of gold and a passport to heaven. It's competition. Constant training. Pain. Disappointment. Weariness at times. Even endless sacrifice.

If you've made it thus far in this book, I assume you have made the choice to live as a spiritual champion. The life of a spiritual champion is not easy. In the heat of competition, everyone learns quickly that it is a tough road. A road of struggle. Challenge. Heartache.

But also victory!

Olympic champions are motivated by inner qualities which most of the world ignores; the same is true of spiritual champions. If we are to step into the winner's circle, it is time to step up the level of our competition. The forecast is positive. When the right things are in place, we don't even need luck. Who needs luck when you have God? As the apostle Paul stated in Romans 8:31, "If God is for us, who is against us?" Even in the heat of competition, God is for us.

What Spiritual Champions Need Most

Many similarities exist between an Olympic champion and a spiritual champion. In this practical section, I want to draw some parallels between the qualities of an Olympic champion that we just considered and those of a spiritual champion. If we implement these qualities, we will be enabled to continue our spiritual championship stride all the way to the finish line— where we'll be crowned by none other than Jesus Christ Himself.

A Vision to Win

> If you have Jesus Christ in your life, you are already a winner. You are not on your way to *becoming* a winner, you are a winner *already*.

Perhaps one of the most remarkable discoveries you will ever make is that if you have Jesus Christ in your life, you are already a winner. You are not on your way to *becoming* a winner, you are a winner *already*. You do not have to prove yourself to anyone. You do not have to perform to gain your worth. God esteems you as a winner if you know His Son personally.

Yet there is a difference between being a member of the winning side and being a champion. All Christians are winners, but not all Christians are spiritual champions.

Think back to ancient Israel. The difference between a winner and a champion is like the difference between a soldier in David's army and one of his "mighty men" listed in 2 Samuel 23:8-39. Every soldier in David's army was a winner, but only a few were called mighty men. How did they earn such a title? By achieving a record that was exemplary, outstanding, unusually excellent. These mighty men went beyond the norm, past the expected, and set their sights on something more. They were winners because they were part of the winning side, but they were champions because they wouldn't settle for anything less than the best.

I wonder: Do you have a vision to excel in the Christian life? Do you see yourself as a champion in your faith? A spiritual champion has a vision to overcome in the Christian life. He sees himself in the winner's circle, raising the banners of victory that bring glory to God's name. In his mind he can hear the strong chords of praise lifted to God as he and other champions exalt the name of Jesus.

Is it like the Olympics? No, it's far better. All the medals and accolades of this world will soon pass away. The cheering fades. The records are broken. But while spiritual champions may not receive the praise of men—they may not even be recognized as significant figures—their rewards are everlasting and the divine cheering section never grows hoarse.

What's important in the end is what God says about you. Spiritual champions see themselves entering the gates of heaven, walking on streets of gold and talking to Paul, Elijah, Moses, Nehemiah, Timothy, and thousands of others whose strong faith has been passed down through many generations. But most of all, spiritual champions see themselves talking to Jesus, receiving His rewards, and then casting them at His feet in worship and adoration.

> " Spiritual champions see themselves entering the gates of heaven, walking on streets of gold and talking to Paul, Elijah, Moses, Nehemiah, Timothy, and thousands of others whose strong faith has been passed down through many generations. "

This ultimate vision of heaven empowers a spiritual champion to envision victory through present difficulties and challenges. He knows the struggle on this side of heaven will one day be worth it all. He knows the Spirit-powered effort which is required to move beyond the level of "winner" to that of "champion" is insignificant compared to the rewards God promises.

Just as an Olympic champion envisions himself crossing the finish line ahead of other world-class athletes, we must envision ourselves as triumphing over Satan, ourselves, and our sin. Yes, even over our circumstances.

Develop that vision to win. See yourself as a champion who defeats his opponents by depending upon the strength and wisdom of the One who calls us into the competition. Even if all hell is breaking loose in your life, remember that spiritual champions fight to win—not in their own strength, but in the power of the Spirit of God. Spiritual champions have a vision to win.

The Fire of the Spirit

Just as an Olympic athlete has a fire or spirit within him to keep him going through the long days of strenuous training, as a spiritual champion, you have the fire of the Holy Spirit within you. He wants to empower you to live the Christian life, to make you a winner.

The moment you accepted Jesus Christ into your life, you received the gift of His Spirit. His Spirit will never leave you. Once you are truly a child of God, you are always a child of God. God never leaves you helpless or friendless. His Spirit abides in you forever.

The empowerment bestowed on us depends solely on allowing the Holy Spirit to fill us daily and control our lives. A surrendered life will result in a God-powered life, rather than a man-powered life.

Every spiritual champion needs a spiritual breakthrough. Our mind, will, and emotions become encrusted like callused feet as we walk through the challenges of life. Our flesh ages by the day, yet continually exercises its dominant power. God has to break through this encrustation before anyone can even know we have Christ in our lives. This is why a spiritual breakthrough is imperative.

This spiritual breakthrough is accomplished as the fire of the Spirit is ignited continually within us. The fire of the Spirit is smothered when we are disobedient and don't bother spending time with God. Being with God daily will fan the flame of the Spirit.

Spiritual champions are motivated by the fire of the Spirit. They are not motivated by the praise of men, even though it's natural to enjoy such praise; the trick is to pass it on to God. The fire of the Spirit is there for us when no one else will be. The Spirit will be pulling for us at all times like the twelfth man, the fans of a football team. He will empower us to stand firm and true in the midst of whatever we face.

We will discover the meaning of a man when we are being empowered by the Spirit. God has destined us to be spiritually powerful men. Anything less is not the will of God. Let's choose today to be men with the fire of the Spirit burning brightly in our lives.

To Bounce Back

Spiritual champions, like all others, will periodically fail in the Christian life. It is not possible or wise to try to live "a pie in the sky in the sweet bye and bye" type of Christian life which never admits failure. A Christian who says he no longer sins and never fails is simply deceived.

One of the keys to the Christian life is learning that it is possible to bounce back even from failure. Disappointment comes when we fail in some area of the Christian life. A real spiritual champion is motivated to move beyond disappointment toward repentance when he fails. A spiritual champion bounces back.

One area in which so many of us fail is spending time daily with God. Spiritual champions earnestly desire to spend time with God, yet circumstances, stress, pressure, and priorities regularly interrupt this. Often when men miss this time with God they get discouraged and down on themselves. They begin to think, *What is the use, anyway?* This can move a man from periodic spiritual failure to continual failure.

How can we deal with this? By bouncing back. Spiritual champions are determined to bounce back even when they know they have not kept their commitments. Giving up accomplishes nothing. It simply plays into the hands of Satan.

I believe God is more concerned about our attitudes toward our sin than

He is sin itself. If our attitude is flippant and smug, God is grieved. But if our attitude is broken and repentant, God delights in showing mercy to us. When our attitude is broken and contrite, we will not sin as often. We will win over sin!

The guys you know who are lost and unchurched are watching how you respond to personal failure. They will want to know the God you know when they see you bounce back. But if they see you beating up on yourself, filled with depression, why should they want your God? They wouldn't—and to tell the truth, neither would I.

Brothers, the fire of the Spirit will empower us to bounce back to the glory of God. So let's allow it to do its great work.

A Goal to Reach

Spiritual champions try hard to keep their goal before them. And what's the goal? The goal of a spiritual champion is to become like Jesus Christ. This will not be completed until Jesus comes again or we die and go to heaven. But in the meantime, spiritual champions are becoming more and more like Jesus. God is working like a sculptor in our lives, chipping away at each area that does not look like Jesus.

Human comparison is difficult to avoid. Our tendency is to gauge how we are doing in our spiritual lives by comparing ourselves to the other men we know. Some even compare their performance with their pastors or some spiritual mentor. But this is a fatal error. It's a great way to deceive ourselves.

Jesus Christ is the only true standard of comparison. He is the one we are supposed to become like. That will become possible as long as we are controlled by the Holy Spirit.

The more we become like Jesus, the more evident it will be to others that God is working in our lives. This is why comparison to others can be deadly. It encourages us to enter a false comfort zone. Looking continually to Jesus, on the other hand, will empower us to become like Him and will send us strides ahead of most men spiritually in the race of life. They will notice the difference Jesus is making in us. When this happens, others will discover through our life that Jesus is the Savior they themselves so desperately need.

Spiritual champions need a goal to reach for, a goal that cannot be reached by mere human effort. They need a goal that is attainable only through the supernatural intervention of God.

A Plan for Trouble

No spiritual champion should set out without a plan for trouble, a road map that can anticipate the setbacks of life. Without question, as long as we are in this flesh, our life will be full of trouble. We are either going into a storm, are in a storm, or are coming out of a storm. Storms are a part of life.

We must be careful not to ask the wrong questions, such as How hard is the wind blowing in my storms? How much more pressure can I take? How many more difficulties can I undertake? Those are the wrong questions. The right question is, How am I going to respond in a Christlike manner in the midst of my difficult circumstances?

Do you remember the story of Shadrach, Meshach, and Abednego in the book of Daniel? All three were placed in the fiery furnace because of their allegiance to God. They refused to worship the idol Nebuchadnezzar had set up. After they were thrown into the furnace, the Lord appeared to them and kept them safe in the flames. Although the soldiers who threw them into the fire were all killed by the heat, not one hair on the heads of these three young men was singed by the fire. Even Nebuchadnezzar was impressed with their God. He knew that no one but their God could have preserved them from harm in the fire.

Let me make two observations from this story. First, Shadrach, Meshach, and Abednego never asked for a change of residence; they simply wanted to find God in the midst of their trouble. Second, God appeared to them. A theophany took place. The Lord literally appeared in their midst. He was their covering and their safety. This tells us a lot about what ought to be in our own plan for trouble.

A spiritual champion's plan for trouble is simple: it's to determine to find God in the midst of trouble. Nothing is more important than this. Spiritual champions want to grow and mature spiritually, and spirituality always calls for God in the midst of circumstances; carnality, on the other hand, always calls for a change in the circumstances.

What spiritual champions need most is to have a plan for trouble. Difficulties will come. You can count on it. Therefore, we must respond in a godly fashion by determining to discover God in the trouble. This is the action of a true spiritual champion.

Perseverance

No spiritual champion makes it to the finish line without perseverance. Without a determination and commitment to complete whatever he has begun, he won't make it. From the very beginning, he must decide that, come what may, he will never quit.

Jesus Christ exemplified true perseverance for each of us. He never quit. It would have been easy to give up when He was facing ridicule, physical abuse, and death. He could have backed off and never been crucified. But He stuck with it. He was determined.

If you're like me, times come when you feel like quitting the Christian life. You wonder if the work it takes to build a successful marriage is worth it. You think life would be a lot simpler and much more enjoyable without the demands of church. You want to walk away from your job or even your career.

Of course, there are some things that perhaps you *should* quit. But it is never right nor wise to quit in your walk with Jesus, your commitment to His church, or your marriage. Those three areas of life need all the resolve that's available. Fortunately, God has promised to supply you with the grit and determination you require. That doesn't mean it will be easy! But winning a championship is never easy. It is, however, worth every ounce of effort it requires.

A real spiritual champion understands that he is called to be a thermostat in his relationships, not a thermometer of his circumstances. The purpose of a thermostat is to set the climate of the room. Spiritual champions set the climate around them when they demonstrate perseverance. The purpose of a thermometer is to reflect or read the climate in the room or in life. Anyone can be a thermometer, but not everyone has perseverance, a "can do" spirit, a never-quit mentality. True spiritual champions never quit.

> A real spiritual champion understands that he is called to be a thermostat in his relationships, not a thermometer of his circumstances.

Taken together, these six qualities are what spiritual champions need most. You may have noticed I left out the seventh criterion for Olympic champions noted in *The Reader's Digest* article. That was intentional. Spiritual champions never "make their own luck." Neither do they look for luck to come from somewhere else. A spiritual champion understands that "luck" goes out the window wherever God is involved. There are no lucky spiritual champions—only divinely protected ones.

And I'll take that any day.

Continuing as a Spiritual Champion

The 1992 Olympic Games featured one of the most dramatic moments in the history of sports. It captured the hearts of people all across the world.

Derek Redmond, a British runner, tore a hamstring in a 400-meter semifinal race and collapsed on the track. After a few excruciating moments, he was able to drag himself back to his feet. A stunned crowd watched breathlessly as he began to hobble toward the finish line. Watching in the stands was his father. Supposing that Derek was attempting to get off of the track, he immediately rushed to help him.

But Derek Redmond did not want to leave the track. He intended to finish the race.

Leaning on his father, Derek began to slowly limp to the finish line. As this remarkable pair inched forward, the crowd erupted in applause, the eyes of spectators around the enormous stadium filled with tears. Each time I see that video clip, I follow the crowd's example. I am moved to tears as I watch that father help his wounded son complete the race.

These moving images provide an appropriate illustration for what God does for you and me. Through the race of life we falter and fail. Yet in the worst of these times, the Father comes to our side and helps us to continue the race, helping us to finish as a spiritual champion. This is the purpose of the Holy Spirit in our lives. He is our Helper. The Bible says in John 16:7, "But I tell you the truth, it is to your advantage that I go away; for if I do not go away, the Helper shall not come to you; but if I go, I will send Him to you."

The Holy Spirit is our Helper. He helps us to grasp the victory that Jesus Christ has already secured for us.

The power of the Holy Spirit is essential in helping us win as spiritual champions. Without His work in us and through us, it would be impossible to become a spiritual champion. The good news for us all is that the Spirit helps us through our weakness. Romans 8:26-27 tells us,

> And in the same way the Spirit also helps our weakness; for we do not know how to pray as we should, but the Spirit Himself intercedes for us with groanings too deep for words; and He who searches the hearts knows what the mind of the Spirit is, because He intercedes for the saints according to the will of God.

Even when we do not know what to pray or how to pray, the Holy Spirit intercedes for us to continue doing the will of God.

The only way to become a spiritual champion is to rely on the Holy Spirit. As we discover that we have been fully empowered to be a spiritual champion, we will find real meaning in life.

STUDY QUESTIONS

1. Do you have "a vision to win"? If so, what is it? What keeps you going?

2. What does Ronnie mean by "the fire of the Spirit"? Why is this important in the life of a spiritual champion? Do you have it? Explain.

3. How easy is it for you to bounce back from adversity? What have you learned during such times?

4. Describe the major spiritual goal you want to reach in your life. How do you plan to reach this goal?

5. Why is it important to plan for trouble? What plans do you have for trouble in the future? Describe them.

6. Are you easily tempted to quit, or do you consider yourself a person of perseverance? Explain.

7. Why doesn't luck play a role in the life of a spiritual champion?

8. Read the story of Derek Redmond at the end of this chapter. Who in your life can help you get back up when you fall in the race of life?

9. Read John 16:7. According to Jesus, why was it a good thing that He was about to go away? How does this "good thing" still assist us today? How is it assisting you?

10. Read Romans 8:26-27. What specific role of the Spirit does this verse explain? How is this helpful? Try to describe a time when the truth of this verse became especially meaningful to you.

PART THREE

How to Lose It

The Opponents of a Spiritual Champion

He was their champion, standing at nine and a half feet tall. His armor tipped the scales at two hundred pounds; the head of his spear alone weighed twenty-five pounds. He was arrogant. Merciless. Intimidating. Without question, he was a giant of a man. His name was Goliath, but everyone just called him "Champ."

For forty days and forty nights this hero of the Philistine army defied the God of Israel. Twice a day Goliath issued a challenge for any man to fight him. This overgrown bully loved to intimidate others by his size and his words.

The army of God feared this Philistine champion. Saul's army had great numbers, but puny faith. They thought Goliath and the Philistines were unbeatable and feared they would soon become their slaves. Saul's army saw Goliath as more god than champion. Not a single Israelite would step forward to face the monster in hand-to-hand combat.

> **Saul's army had great numbers, but puny faith. Not a single Israelite would step forward to face the monster in hand-to-hand combat.**

But then a young shepherd boy named David came to the battlefield to bring food to his elder brothers who served in the Israeli army. Unknown to most, God had anointed this young man to be the next king of Israel. Up until this day, David had spent most of his time taking care of sheep and playing the harp for King Saul.

When he arrived on the battlefield, David longed to be part of the action. Standing near the front lines, he heard Goliath curse and defy the God of Israel. Such insolence infuriated David. He demanded to know who this uncircumcised Philistine thought he was to taunt the armies of the living God. David was anxious to fight this champion.

He went immediately to King Saul and asked for permission to face Goliath. Saul reminded David of his youth and that Goliath had been a great warrior all of his life. But David wouldn't back down. He wanted this champion; He felt sure God would deliver the giant into his hands. No doubt Saul and the others who heard David thought he was just a young and foolish boy, yet they couldn't deny his courage. Neither could they deny his past accomplishments:

> "Your servant has killed both the lion and the bear; and this uncircumcised Philistine will be like one of them, since he has taunted the armies of the living God." And David said, "The LORD who delivered me from the paw of the lion and from the paw of the bear, He will deliver me from the hand of the Philistine." And Saul said to David, "Go, and may the LORD be with you." [1 Samuel 17:36-37]

David did not applaud his own strength or ability, but spoke confidently of how God would deliver him from Goliath. He knew that if God had given him the strength to defeat the lion and the bear, this same God would give him the strength to defeat the Philistine.

David prepared himself for battle by taking five stones and his sling, along with the name of his God. Saul attempted to suit him up with armor, but David did not want it or need it. He had his God.

What confidence, courage, and boldness this young man displayed! Underline in the following passage the places that demonstrate his confidence. First Samuel 17:45-52 says,

> Then David said to the Philistine, "You come to me with a sword, a spear, and a javelin, but I come to you in the name of the LORD of hosts, the God of the armies of Israel, whom you have taunted. This day the LORD will deliver you up into my hands, and I will strike you down and remove your head from you. And I will give the dead bodies of the army of the Philistines this day to the birds of the sky and the wild beasts of the earth, that all the earth may know there is a God in Israel, and that all this assembly may know that the LORD does not deliver by sword or by spear; for the battle is the LORD's and He will give you into our hands."
>
> Then it happened when the Philistine rose and came and drew near to meet David, that David ran quickly toward the battle line to meet the Philistine. And David put his hand into his bag and took from it a stone and slung it, and struck the Philistine on his forehead. And the stone sank into his forehead, so that he fell on his face to the ground. Thus David prevailed over the Philistine with a sling and a stone, and he struck the Philistine and killed him; but there was no sword in David's hand. Then David ran and stood over the Philistine and took his sword and drew it out of its sheath and killed him, and cut off his head with it. When the Philistines saw that their champion was dead, they fled. And the men of Israel and Judah arose and shouted and pursued the Philistines as far as the

valley, and to the gates of Ekron. And the slain Philistines lay along the way to Shaaraim, even to Gath and Ekron.

Isn't that one of the most exciting passages anywhere in the Bible?

The Philistines' dreaded champion was dead. No longer would he taunt armies of God. David would not stand for it. He knew the battle was the Lord's and he pursued Goliath to the death. When Goliath was killed, the Philistines ran for cover. The army of God pursued them and prevailed . . . all because of a young shepherd boy who refused to be intimidated by the size and words of Goliath.

What was the major difference between Goliath and David? Goliath was a mere champion. David was a *spiritual* champion. In 1 Samuel 17:4,23,51, Goliath is referred to as a champion. Yet he lost. Goliath had great size and strength; David had a great God. Goliath used words as his weapon of intimidation; David had the name of God. The bottom line: Goliath dead . . . David alive!

The practical applications from this story are numerous. But at this point I want to make an observation that no spiritual champion can afford to forget: *Champions are not determined by the size of their bodies, but by the size of their God.*

> *Champions are not determined by the size of their bodies, but by the size of their God.*

Body strength can be helpful. The macho look may impress a few. Words can be as strong as Goliath's and a man may be the king of his world just as Goliath ruled his.

But so what? You are going down if you don't have God. Any little pebble could do the trick.

The Lord is the only hope we have. The power we have as men, as spiritual champions, is found only in the name of our God. All else is futile. Vain. Powerless.

True spiritual champions are not determined by their size, but by the size of their God. Our God is the key to our victory. He is big. The word "awesome" ought to be reserved only for Him. He is an awesome God! Mighty. Strong. Omnipotent.

That's good for us, because every spiritual champion will face some fierce opponents. Everyone wants to bring down a champion. Many well-known spiritual champions have fallen in our day and their failure has rocked the Christian world. Still other spiritual champions falter and fail daily. Why? What's the main reason for their fall? It's this: *Any spiritual champion who loses a battle or a war to one of his opponents does so by making the same mistake Goliath made—He trusts in his own strength.*

A spiritual champion falls when he becomes confident in his own look, his own words, his own ability. The moment this occurs, defeat lies just around the corner.

Let me say it again: The size of our God is the key to not losing a battle or a war as a spiritual champion. All we really need is God. Nothing and no one else—just Him. Remember, that is all David had. He didn't have two hundred pounds of armor, a twenty-five-pound spearhead, massive biceps, or a chest full of war decorations. Goliath had all these things, and he lost. David had none of them, but he did have God. Yet he was the only one standing at the end of the battle.

God is all we need. When we believe and practice this, we will be able to overcome even the fiercest of our opponents.

The Fiercest Opponents of a Spiritual Champion

Spiritual champions lose when they underestimate the power of their enemies. Spiritual champions also lose when they go into battle unprepared.

So what's the best preparation for defeating our opponents? Get to know them. Discover the truth about them. That's the way to prepare for battle. Spiritual champions have three fierce opponents. Let's take a look at them one by one.

Satan

Satan is the fiercest of our opponents. In reality, he is our only opponent. The other two we'll consider are mere underlings; he's the real deal.

> " Satan is the fiercest of our opponents. In reality, he is our only opponent. "

Since Satan is our fiercest opponent and the source of all other opposition, let's investigate what we might be able to learn about him. Ephesians 6:10-12 tells us,

> Finally, be strong in the LORD, and in the strength of His might. Put on the full armor of God, that you may be able to stand firm against the schemes of the devil. For our struggle is not against flesh and blood, but against the rulers, against the powers, against the world forces of this darkness, against the spiritual forces of wickedness in the heavenly places.

We are in a war with Satan. Every day we live for Jesus we are in a war against demonic forces. Satan is our enemy.

When the Bible says we are in a struggle with Satan, it means that we are in hand-to-hand combat with him. Do you ever feel weary? As if you have been in a battle—yet you have no recollection of a literal firefight? Most of us have this sense, and it's real. It's real because we really have been in a battle; we've been engaging in spiritual warfare. Make no mistake about it, we have been in a real battle. Scripture makes it clear just how real the battle can be.

1. Satan's origin. Where did Satan come from? The Bible says in Ezekiel 28:12-17,

Son of man, take up a lamentation over the king of Tyre, and say to him, Thus says the Lord GOD, "You had the seal of perfection, full of wisdom and perfect in beauty. You were in Eden, the garden of God; Every precious stone was your covering . . . . You were the anointed cherub who covers, and I placed you there. You were on the holy mountains of God; You walked in the midst of the stones of fire. You were blameless in your ways from the day you were created, until unrighteousness was found in you. By the abundance of your trade you were internally filled with violence, and you sinned; therefore, I have cast you as profane from the mountain of God. And I have destroyed you, O covering cherub, from the midst of the stones of fire. Your heart was lifted up because of your beauty; You corrupted your wisdom by reason of your splendor. I cast you to the ground; I put you before kings, that they may see you."

Satan was once an angel of God named Lucifer. He had a special anointing in heaven to lead the angels in worship of God. The Bible says in Isaiah 14:12-15,

"How you have fallen from heaven, O star of the morning, son of the dawn! You have been cut down to the earth, you have weakened the nations! But you said in your heart, 'I will ascend to heaven; I will raise my throne above the stars of God, and I will sit on the mount of assembly in the recesses of the north. I will ascend above the heights of the clouds; I will make myself like the Most High.' Nevertheless you will be thrust down to Sheol, to the recesses of the pit."

It was not good enough for Lucifer to lead all of heaven in worship. He wanted to be worshiped as God. He led a rebellion in heaven against God. It is believed that one-third of the angels bought into the lies of Lucifer. God kicked them out of heaven and prepared for them a place called hell. These angels who fell with Lucifer are his demons. Lucifer is Satan.

"Satan" means adversary, opponent, and enemy. "Devil" means slanderer. Satan is our opponent. Just as he slandered God in heaven, he continues to slander us today. This is the origin of Satan.

2. *Satan's organization.* Satan is more organized than the Mafia. We must remember that we are not going into hand-to-hand combat with other people or our circumstances. We are going into daily combat with an organized, powerful, intelligent schemer named Satan.

Ephesians 6:12 tells us something about the organization of Satan. Satan is the commander-in-chief of all the demonic armies. Every demon answers to him. I believe the term "rulers" is a reference to specific demons that serve as commanding generals over the nations of the world and that every nation of the world has been assigned a demon. The book of Daniel seems to support this in its last few chapters.

What I'm about to say may take some of you by surprise, but I believe there is a chief demon assigned over America. His goal is to destroy this nation. He uses his demonic forces to execute the ultimate purpose of Satan. It is time we got our eyes off one another or some group that tends to differ from us and train them on the real enemy. Our enemy is not any particular group or political party; our enemy is Satan.

I believe Ephesians 6:12 also teaches there are "admirals" who serve in Satan's armies. These "powers" attack us continually. The real work horses of Satan's armies are his "sergeants" who are the "world forces of darkness" in this verse. These tenacious demons work around the clock bringing destruction. Satan's ground forces, the privates in his army, are "the spiritual forces of wickedness." Daily these demons do battle with us. They're active whether we're aware of their activities or not. So wouldn't it be better to be aware of what they're up to?

This battle is taking place in the heavenly places. According to Ephesians 1:3 and 2:6, we are seated in the heavenly places. Therefore, we are to do battle in the heavenly places with Satan and his demons. How do we do this? By praying in the Spirit. Prayer places us in a strategic position to do battle.

Satan is very powerful, far more powerful than we are in our flesh. But he's no match for God! Satan is not omnipotent, omnipresent, or omniscient. Only God is omnipotent, omnipresent, and omniscient. And that's why our victory is assured!

The Lust of the Flesh and Lust of the Eyes

Our second great enemy does not attack us from without, but from within. Ever since Adam, men have battled an incredible desire to fulfill the desires of the flesh and their eyes. First John 2:15-17 says,

> Do not love the world, nor the things in the world. If anyone loves the world, the love of the Father is not in him. For all that is in the world, the lust of the flesh and the lust of the eyes and the boastful pride of life, is not from the Father, but is from the world. And the world is passing away, and also its lusts; but the one who does the will of God abides forever.

The lust of the flesh is the ravenous desire of our fleshly appetites to be satisfied. Yet the desire of the flesh is insatiable. It does not matter how much we attempt to gratify the flesh, it is never sated.

Once we yield to it, it only wants more.

What are the works of the flesh? Galatians 5:19-21 tells us,

> Now the deeds of the flesh are evident, which are: immorality, im-

purity, sensuality, idolatry, sorcery, enmities, strife, jealousy, out-
bursts of anger, disputes, dissensions, factions, envying, drunken-
ness, carousing, and things like these, of which I forewarn you just
as I have forewarned you that those who practice such things shall
not inherit the kingdom of God.

Each of these works of the flesh are desires that cannot ever be fulfilled.
Nothing is ever enough! We can never satisfy the flesh. It will always crave
more. The moment someone tolerates one semi-sex scene in a movie, the
next he will tolerate an explicit sex scene. The moment he tolerates this in
one movie, he will desire to see more scenes like it (only a little more raunchy
this time). Then, in short order, his own sex life will become tainted and
soiled. That isn't what he had in mind when he began with the one ques-
tionable movie scene—but that's the nature of the flesh. It's never satisfied.

Spiritual champions need to recognize that the lust of the flesh and of
the eyes is one of Satan's most popular (and successful) strategies. They must
beware of drawing too close to the line or they will find themselves crossing
it.

I am convinced that this opponent is destroying the lives of men and
their families as much as any. This strategy of Satan is sometimes subtle, at
other times very blatant. It doesn't seem to matter; men fall prey to both.

Guys, it does not have to be this way. We don't have to give in to the
lust of our flesh and eyes. Spiritual champions have a resource unavailable
to the non-believer. If the Holy Spirit lives within us, the excuse that "I'm
only human" no longer applies. We have been given divine resources that enable us to live supernatural lives. And the only way we'll be able to stand
against the wiles of the devil is by tapping into those resources every moment
of every day.

The Pride of Life

I believe pride is the basis of all sin. Anytime I worship myself, exalt myself, I am a victim of pride. Pride is self-centered. How appropriate that the
middle letter in the word pride is "I."

In the last week of my forty days of prayer and fasting, God seized my
attention late one evening and into the early morning with a startling passage
of Scripture. God forced me to contend with Isaiah 57:15.

For thus says the high and exalted One who lives forever, whose
name is Holy, "I dwell on a high and holy place, and also with the
contrite and lowly of spirit in order to revive the spirit of the lowly
and to revive the heart of the contrite."

In this verse God convicted me greatly that I was a man of pride. I had
been so deceived by Satan that I had allowed him to build a stronghold of
pride in my life. I suddenly saw that *my* interests and *my* goals and *my* desires

and *my* best were always the priorities in my life. I thought I had surrendered all to Christ, but I was deceived. In this experience God gave new light to me, tearing away the shadows and illuminating my pride in all its ugliness.

I had to be broken. I had to repent. I had to let the Lord strike pride from my life. And He did it! Through this experience the Lord broke through in my life in a brand new way. I know there are lessons yet to learn and fleshly tendencies still to crucify, but in this experience God brought fresh release to my soul, setting me free from myself and my selfish desires.

Don't let it slip your attention that the New Testament twice warns us that God opposes the proud but gives grace to the humble (*see* James 4:6; 1 Peter 5:5). The good news is that God is committed to showing us our great need to be men of humility and repentance. When we allow this to occur, we can expect the "grace" to be multiplied. This is what I want in my life more than anything.

Watch out! Pride is a fierce opponent. It will rob you of spiritual power. It will de-throne you as a spiritual champion more quickly than almost anything else. Pride is the root of all sin. Yet when we realize its deadly grip on our own lives and repent of it, we find ourselves quickly propelled to a new spiritual plane. Such is the grace and mercy of our loving God.

Strategies for Overcoming Our Opponents

Our opponents are so cunning, so strong, so implacable. Can they be overcome? Absolutely! In fact, through Jesus Christ the opponents—Satan, the lust of the flesh and eyes, and the pride of life—have already been defeated. Oh, they're not dead quite yet. They can still cause a great deal of mischief. But Jesus has already triumphed over them through the cross, and when we abide in the power of the cross, we share in His victory.

Let's return for a moment to the life of David. His story teaches us at least two ways to overcome our enemies. In the same way that he defeated champion Goliath, spiritual champions can defeat their opponents.

Understand Your Spiritual Position

Just as David understood that God had a great plan for his life—he had been anointed by God to be the next king of Israel—we must understand that God has a great plan for our lives. David understood his position with God; we must understand our position in Christ. Just as David was destined to be a spiritual champion, we are destined to be spiritual champions through Jesus Christ.

When David rose up against Goliath, he did not come in the power of his flesh. No doubt he had great flesh. But David came in the name of the Lord. Goliath came with a spear, a sword, and a javelin; all David

> **Spiritual champions do not need weapons of the flesh. We have the name of Jesus, the most powerful name in heaven and on earth. What else do we need?**

needed was the name of God. Through the name of God, David understood his spiritual position. He knew he was a spiritual champion.

Spiritual champions do not need weapons of the flesh. We do not need what men see as power. We have the name of Jesus, the most powerful name in heaven and on earth. What else do we need?

When Satan attacks you, call out the name of Jesus. When the lusts of your flesh and eyes are drawing you into fulfilling the temptation of the moment, speak forth boldly the name of Jesus. When pride exalts itself through your life, the name of Jesus can shatter it in a moment. The name of Jesus places us in the heavenly places and ensures spiritual victory and power.

Spiritual champions are unconcerned about a name for themselves. They are concerned about lifting up the name of Jesus. This is why when we pray in the name of Jesus, we are accessing all of heaven's blessings upon your life. Let's live, pray, and operate in the name of Jesus. There is no other name like the name of Jesus. He is the Savior of the world!

Claim Your Spiritual Victory

David announced publicly that God was his deliverer. He understood that the battle with Goliath wasn't his, but God's. It may not have looked like it, but it was really a spiritual battle. As David stepped toward Goliath, he exercised faith in the God of Israel. This was the same God who had delivered him earlier in his life from the bear and the lion. David claimed his spiritual victory and God gave it to him. Spiritual champions always claim their victories.

Now is the time for you as a spiritual champion to announce to your opponents that the Lord is your deliverer. Satan needs to be reminded of it, your flesh and eyes need to know it, and pride needs to be rebuked continually. If you are going to claim your victory as a spiritual champion, you need to be confident in the Lord alone as your Deliverer. You cannot deliver yourself from any of your opponents. So stop trying. God wants you to claim that He is your Deliverer.

Spiritual champions understand that every battle they face is the Lord's battle. Whatever you are facing today in your life, remember that the battle is the Lord's. Let Him fight for you. When the Lord fights the battle, He always wins. Let God fight all of your battles. If the God of David can defeat champion Goliath, the Goliaths you face in your life can also be slain.

> **Let God fight all of your battles. If the God of David can defeat champion Goliath, the Goliaths you face in your life can also be slain.**

To use a biblical phrase, the Lord will give them into your hands!

You are a spiritual champion. I urge you to ponder your spiritual position and claim your spiritual victory today. Whoever and whatever opposes you, stand against your adversaries and your problems. Your opponents may be fierce, but your God is great! You can overcome all of your opponents because Jesus Christ has already defeated each of them. Now it's up to you to remind them of the fact.

S T U D Y   Q U E S T I O N S

1. What kind of opponents do you have to face in living out the Christian life?

2. Ronnie writes, "Champions are not determined by the size of their bodies, but by the size of their God." What does he mean? And why is this important?

3. Read Ephesians 6:10-12 and 1 Peter 5:8. What do you learn about Satan from these verses? What action is required on our part? Are you taking such action? Explain.

4. What does it mean to "pray in the Spirit"? Is this a practice of yours? Why or why not?

5. Read John 2:15-17. What dangers are listed here? How are we to respond to them? Which of them are hardest for you to deal with? Why?

6. Read Galatians 5:19-21. Which of these sins give you the most trouble? Which do you struggle least with? How are you dealing with the most difficult areas?

7. Why do you think Ronnie writes that "I believe pride is the basis of all sin"? How does this fit with Isaiah 57:15?

8. Read James 4:6 and 1 Peter 5:5. How does God respond to pride? How does He respond to humility? Which does he respond to most often in your own life?

9. Imagine that you had to explain your spiritual position to a brand new Christian. What would you say?

10. What does it mean to "claim your spiritual victory"? How can you do this? Are you doing this? Explain.

＊＊＊

CHAPTER   TEN

How to Forfeit a
Spiritual Championship

I spent the first thirty years of my life in Texas. My home state is known for many things: its beautiful bluebonnets, varied terrain, Mexican food, high school football, hot summer temperatures, the petroleum industry, and the Alamo. Texas is also known for its snakes—especially rattlesnakes.

Rattlesnake roundups take place throughout the state each year. Large groups gather in snake attire to see who can catch the largest rattlesnake. Now, every Texan knows that it only takes one bite from a rattlesnake to kill you. The thrill of danger and taking that risk motivates men and women to participate in this unusual "sport."

Rattlesnakes come in many shapes and sizes. They can extend great lengths (taller than an average man), or they can grow fat (as big around as your arm). These vipers boast a number of rattles on the tip of their tails. These rattles begin to shake just before the snake strikes. Any Texan knows you're in serious trouble should you hear that distinctive sound.

If a rattlesnake successfully locks its fangs to any area of your body and you survive the strike, that part of your body may be numb for the rest of your life. The poison has the power to kill or, at the very least, to maim a person. Once bitten, you are in a race with time. Immediate action must be taken. No one takes a rattlesnake bite lightly; life hangs in the balance as the deadly poison surges through the body.

As a young boy I learned about the rattlesnake. Some of my closest relatives lived in the country. When we visited this family on the farm, we children would usually be warned to watch out for snakes, especially if one had been spotted or killed recently. Through these dire warnings, I developed a great respect for the reptile. In fact, for all snakes.

Let me be candid. I hate snakes! It doesn't matter what kind, size, or color they are, or whether they are poisonous or not. I cannot stand even to look at them. In my childhood, especially after returning from that hot and dusty farm, I would suffer frightful nightmares of snakes surrounding my bed. I would wake in terror, frozen in fear. More than once I have heard family members recount the ordeals of my nightmares.

I know that Moses and I have at least one attribute in common. When Moses threw down his rod and it turned into a snake, the Bible says that he fled. A kindred spirit! Whenever I see a snake of any kind, I flee. I run as fast as I can. I will trample over anything or anyone to escape it.

I am thankful that to this day, rattlesnakes have not played a major role in my life. I have seen them after they've been killed by someone else, but I have never (so far as I know) had a close call by unintentionally walking up on one of the critters. I pray I never will.

Rest assured that if I ever did come upon a rattlesnake, I would not reach down and pick it up. I would not caress it gently and say, "You are such a pretty little thing. You are such a nice snake. I love your fangs. Your rattlers are so large. Your skin is so soft. Nice snake. Yes, nice snake." I would not allow the rattlesnake to slither all around my body as I talked to it and handled it like it was a docile, harmless pet. I can promise you this would never happen. If it did, you can be sure death would be imminent. If not by snakebite, by heart attack.

You may think all this rattlesnake phobia is needless, but allow me to draw a comparison. Today, men are picking up rattlesnakes all around them. They are entertaining them, caressing them, tolerating them, gazing at them, touching them, kissing them, and some are even having sex with them. Some men no longer respect the deadly potential of rattlesnakes. They think they can play with them and never get hurt.

> " The kind of rattlesnakes some men are handling—sin—may well choke the life of God from them. "

They don't realize that handling rattlesnakes may cost them their spiritual championship. Real rattlesnakes? No, they can only take physical life. But the kind of rattlesnakes some men are handling—sin—may well choke the life of God from them.

Whenever someone looks upon another woman in a lustful manner, he is picking up a rattlesnake and saying, "Pretty little rattlesnake." When he begins to share his life with a woman other than his wife, he is saying, "You are such a nice rattlesnake. No one understands me like you do."

When he goes to the movie theater and watches some movie where nudity or sexual intercourse are explicitly shown, he is saying, "I love to watch rattlesnakes. They are so beautiful and harmless." When he begins to rent pornographic videos and bring them into his home, he is saying, "Rattlesnakes will not hurt me. No one else will ever know how much I like for them to come into my home and sit on my sofa with me."

When he pads his expense account or cheats on his tax return, he is saying, "I do not know why everyone thinks that rattlesnakes are so bad. I do not see any harm in them." When he enters into a business relationship with a person who does not share his convictions and values he is saying, "I don't see any harm at all in holding rattlesnakes. In fact, I kind of like it."

Whenever a man chooses his own way over God's way, he is saying, "I will follow the rattlesnake all the way to its den." If we willingly disobey God, we are saying, "I don't think that rattlesnakes will really hurt me."

When we admire ourselves to such a degree that we think more highly of ourselves than we ought to think, we are saying, "Oh, I have never seen a rattlesnake like you. I am so gifted and handsome. Come closer and let me see you." When we are so caught up in all of our success, counting the nickels and noses in our profession and through this attempting to obtain some worth, we are saying, "Let me look at you closely, Mr. Rattlesnake. I have never seen a snake with such rattlers. Your fangs are so long. The design on your back is exquisite."

Does all this snake talk sound ridiculous to you? I hope not because it represents reality. There are a lot of men out there who are playing with rattlesnakes. You may even be one of them.

Rattlesnakes Can't Be Tamed

Sin is a far deadlier rattlesnake than any slithering serpent in Texas. But they do have one thing in common: Neither can be tamed. You can't play with either one and expect to live.

Whatever the sin may be or wherever the sin may occur, it is a deadly rattlesnake. The moment you embrace it, you are picking up a rattlesnake, forgetting its deadly venom. There is no such thing as little sin or big sin. Even the size of a Texas rattlesnake does not determine the potency of its venom. In fact, a small rattlesnake at times may be far more deadly than a Texas-size one.

> There is no such thing as little sin or big sin. Even the size of a Texas rattlesnake does not determine the potency of its venom.

We should not entertain sin in our lives anymore than we would a rattlesnake. The result will always be the same: Death! And if not death, the part of our body the snake bites may be numb forever. This is the way sin operates. Wherever it bites, it brings numbness and eventual death. We may never fully recover. Even though sin can be forgiven, its consequences can be permanent.

Rattlesnakes and sin have a lot in common. One of these things is that neither is a respecter of persons. It does not matter who you are or what your gifts may be, rattlesnakes and sin will both strike in a moment's notice. Godliness gives no immunity from the venom. If either locks its fangs on to your life, the consequences will be serious—maybe even fatal.

There is one important way that sin and rattlesnakes differ. Unlike rattlesnakes, sin doesn't sound the alarm before striking. It's far more cunning and deadly than the rattlesnake. It bites with no warning at all.

We should no more entertain or embrace sin than rattlesnakes. The moment we do, it will lock on to us and choke the very life of God out of us. It will destroy us. Perhaps even our family. The moment a man entertains sin, it strikes him. Neither rattlesnakes nor sin are pets. So let's treat sin for what it is, an enemy.

> The best way to lose our spiritual championship is by embracing sin, rather than running from it. Every day men forfeit their spiritual lives because they treat sin like it is a friend.

The best way to lose our spiritual championship standing is by embracing sin, rather than running from it. Every day men forfeit their spiritual lives because they treat sin like it is a friend. The next thing they know, they are losing their families, their jobs, their careers, their friends, or all of them at once.

As spiritual champions, we cannot lose the salvation that God gave us. What He does, He does completely. But what we can lose is the power to gain the spiritual championship that Christ has enabled us to obtain. A spiritual champion can forfeit these benefits, just like a sports champion or a corporate champion can fall from top position. The moment a man begins to make up new rules or ignore the established rules of the game, he can lose the opportunity to become a spiritual champion.

Ways to Forfeit Spiritual Championship Living

Spiritual champions are made—and unmade—every day. How does a man lose his championship status? By making poor choices at some critical point in his life. Most of us struggle to do what is right, but poor choices too often carry devastating consequences. In my second book, *Choices*, I explained that poor choices result in limited spiritual power, counterfeit success, and broken relationships. When a man makes these kinds of poor choices, he forfeits spiritual championship living.

I believe there are three major ways men forfeit spiritual championship living.

Moral Weakness

One of the greatest champions of the Old Testament forfeited his spiritual championship because he consistently made poor moral choices. He caressed the rattlesnake, and he lost.

Samson was a Nazarite. The Nazarite observed three main restrictions in life.[1] First, he was to abstain from wine, vinegar, grape juice, and grapes. Second, he was not to get close to a corpse. Third, he was not to have his hair shaved, because long hair was considered a symbol of strength and vitality.

Samson's birth was a miracle of God. He was destined to be a deliverer of his people. He had tremendous potential to become a mighty spiritual champion—but he was weak morally.

Samson lived on the edge of the rules and one day it caught up with him. (It always does.) In the sixteenth chapter of Judges, we read how Samson forfeited his destiny as a spiritual champion. The Philistines greatly oppressed the people of God and needed to find a way to neutralize this man Samson, who had been a thorn in their sides. Eventually they enticed a beautiful woman named Delilah to seduce Samson and find out where he received his mighty spiritual strength. She called upon all her feminine wiles to trip up Samson and discover his sacred secret.

She finally succeeded. Samson told Delilah that God gave him great strength through his long hair. While he was sleeping, Delilah arranged to have his hair cut. Then she called out to the Philistines to attack him. Samson rose from sleep, expecting to overcome his enemies as before, but this time his strength had vanished. His enemies took him prisoner and gouged out his eyes. He lost it all . . . for the thrill of illicit sexual pleasure.

Samson's problem? Moral weakness. He lived on the edge of the rules once too often. He thought he had sexual intercourse with Delilah; he was too blind to see he had snuggled up to a rattlesnake. God gave him over to his choices, and those poor choices cost him his spiritual power.

> **Samson lived on the edge of the rules once too often. He thought he had sexual intercourse with Delilah; he was too blind to see he had snuggled up to a rattlesnake.**

Disobedience

Saul was the first king of Israel. He forfeited his spiritual championship by choosing to disobey God.

First Samuel 15 tells how Samuel instructed Saul that God wanted the king to go to Amalek and destroy the best of everything. He went to Amalek, all right, and killed its men—but he decided to save some of the best spoil. When Samuel found Saul, the old prophet rebuked him for not fulfilling the will of God. As a result, Saul was rejected as king over Israel. From that point on, Saul's life was filled with tension. Ultimately, he was wounded in battle and fell on his own sword and died.

Disobedience may seem a small thing to us. Certainly, Saul's did to him. But disobedience to God is never a small thing. If you don't believe it, just ask Saul. It cost him his spiritual championship. Saul was so blind he failed to see that his own will was nothing less than a rattlesnake coiled up in the corner of his heart. He forfeited everything just to satisfy his own stubborn will, rather than the will of God.

Pride

Have you ever heard of a man named Nebuchadnezzar? He was king over all of ancient Babylon. Nebuchadnezzar became so enamored with himself that it cost him a spiritual championship. His kind of pride always leads to one thing: destruction.

Nebuchadnezzar loved gold and spread it throughout Babylon. Eventually he created an enormous image of gold and commanded everyone to bow down and worship it. I believe he intended to deify himself publicly. Daniel 4 describes what happened to Nebuchadnezzar next. Daniel warned the king about his pride, but his self-worship continued with arrogant boasting about all he had built in Babylon. The next thing Nebuchadnezzar knew, he was out in the fields, eating grass like a cow. God judged him publicly.

God does not share His glory with anyone. Not even kings. When Nebuchadnezzar embraced pride and hurried to feed his ego, sin struck his life like a rattlesnake. He began to die a very slow death. His life unraveled before everyone's eyes. Whoever lifts himself up publicly, God will take down publicly.

Greater men than you and I have fallen prey to moral weakness, disobedience, and pride. They are all rattlesnakes, and their venom is deadly. If we're not careful, they will take us down more quickly than we can imagine. But we don't have to let that happen.

How to Avoid Forfeiting Your Spiritual Championship

It is possible for all of us to live as a spiritual champion. We do not have to forfeit our spiritual championship on the altars of moral weakness, disobedience, or pride. There are two keys that, used together, will enable us to avoid forfeiting our spiritual championship.

Know the Rules of Life

The rules of life are found in the Bible. The words and principles of the Bible always lead to life. They will never mislead us. They contain no partial truth or error because they are words from God.

If we want to know the rules of life, we must read the Bible. All of us need a plan for reading the Word of God. It's wise to highlight the spiritual principles we find there, then receive and recognize them as being from God. God is perfect and so are His principles.

Live by the Rules of Life

Most Christian men are familiar with the rules of life found in the Bible. Even an atheist can know the rules of life; the greater challenge is living by them. The rules God gives to us are our parameters. As long as we live within these parameters, we can win and keep our spiritual championship.

Samson, Saul, and Nebuchadnezzar all knew the rules of life. God had made the rules plain to them. Yet each wrongly believed God would make an exception for them. We know what happened. Everyone plays by the same rulebook, the Bible. And everyone is responsible to live by the principles that are found there.

You can avoid forfeiting your spiritual championship by knowing the rules of life and living by them. These rules or principles are truth. They will always lead you to life and peace.

Keep the Door Shut!

An aunt and uncle of mine lived on a farm in Southwest Texas, a dusty land filled with cactus. While I was growing up, my family often spent holidays on that farm.

It seemed every time we went out to play, someone would yell to us, "Be careful and watch out for rattlesnakes." Sometimes they described the most recent rattlesnake that had been killed. They would recount the entire event, emphasizing the size of the rattlesnake. I was always anxious to heed their warnings!

Everyone at the farm entered the house through the back door. An enclosed porch served as a utility room, and we would enter the back door, go through the utility room, and then into the kitchen area where most of the family often sat.

A few years ago, my aunt and uncle's son-in-law was walking through the utility room when he heard something behind the washer and dryer. When he leaned over to check out the noise, a rattlesnake bit him. Because he was so quickly rushed to the hospital, he survived.

No one knows how the rattlesnake got into the house. We suppose someone must have left the door open. While the door was open, the rattlesnake took the opportunity to slither into the house and make himself at home. How long had the rattlesnake been there? No one knows—but obviously too long!

What did my relatives learn from this? *Keep the door shut!* Always make sure it is tightly closed, because you never know when another rattlesnake may be slithering by, looking for a new home.

Of course, after this incident no one said, "Nice little snake. Come over here and let me pet you. Why don't you take the master bedroom tonight? If you want, you can crawl into bed with us." They did what you are supposed to do to rattlesnakes: They killed it!

Men, is the door of your life shut? Is the door to your family shut? Is the door to your church shut? What about the door to your business or career? If you do not keep the door shut, the rattlesnakes of life will come in and you won't even know it.

If you do not keep the door shut to your mind, heart, and life, the rattlesnakes of life will come in and hide in the dark recesses of your heart. One day, when you least expect it, they will reach up and strike

> If you do not keep the door shut to your mind, heart, and life, the rattlesnakes of life will come in and hide in the dark recesses of your heart. One day, when you least expect it, they will reach up and strike you.

you. Their goal is to kill you. The moment you open your life to anything that is not godly, you are opening the door to a rattlesnake.

- When you entertain anything that is sensual, you are opening the door to a rattlesnake.
- When you open the door to wrong feelings and don't deal with them, you are opening the door to a rattlesnake.
- When you believe you are really something, you are opening the door to a rattlesnake.
- When you disobey God or His Word, you are opening the door to a rattlesnake.

The moment you entertain any of these things, realize that you are about to be bitten. That is what rattlesnakes do; that's their nature. And when they strike, they bite so quickly you can do very little about it.

Search your life. Are you entertaining rattlesnakes? Do not caress them, get rid of them. The moment you get comfortable with them, they will strike and you will eventually forfeit your standing as a spiritual champion.

Spiritual champions are unwilling to forfeit their great standing. They understand this is their God-given destiny. They know the importance of keeping the door shut. That's the only sure way to keep out the rattlesnakes!

S T U D Y   Q U E S T I O N S

1. What makes rattlesnakes so dangerous? Have you ever "met" one? If so, describe the encounter.

2. What "pretty little rattlesnakes" seem most tempting to you? How do you deal with them?

3. Why is it important to remember that rattlesnakes can't be tamed?

4. Ronnie writes, "There is one important way that sin and rattlesnakes differ. Unlike rattlesnakes, sin doesn't sound the alarm before striking. It's far more cunning and deadly than the rattlesnake. It bites with no warning at all." Have you found this to be true in your own experience? Explain.

5. Ronnie writes that "we can lose . . . the power to gain the spiritual championship that Christ has enabled us to obtain." Do you agree with him? Why or why not?

6. Ronnie lists "moral weakness" as one of the biggest "rattlesnakes" that brings down spiritual champions. Would this be true for you? Explain.

7. Read 1 Samuel 15:22-23. What was the rattlesnake that brought down Saul? How is God's opinion of this rattlesnake often different from our own?

8. How does a person get to "know the rules of life"? Where are they to be found? How familiar are you with these rules?

9. What causes us to stray away from living by the rules of life? How do we know that we have done so?

10. How can you "keep the door shut" when it comes to the rattlesnakes of sin?

PART FOUR

How to Use It

CHAPTER ELEVEN

The Courage of a Spiritual Champion

Where are the great world leaders in our day?

USA Snapshots reports that people believe our country enjoyed its best leadership in the 1960s and 1980s. The same report said that only 8.4 percent of the experts considered that America's best leadership occurred in the 1990s.[1] This lack of confidence in American leadership also exists internationally. Just where are the great leaders in the world today?

In a 1994 meeting called "The Gathering," journalist and former senior correspondent for *Time*, David Aikman, made some interesting remarks. He said,

> There is now a missing sense of purpose of American leadership in the world . . . it grows out of the collapse of the Cold War but far more important, it grows out of what is happening in the grassroots of this country. We are living in a time of a great cultural war. Many Christians think the way to respond to this is to win at the political level . . . in my view, that is only a small part . . . the destiny of nations is decided not by political parties but by what goes on in the culture. What has to be done in this country, not only for international leadership but frankly for the viability of the American constitutional system, is a reformation of culture . . . a re-creation of culture . . . . The place to start is among Christians . . . . Their lives must reflect a serious cultural difference from the rest of a pagan society.[2]

I believe Aikman is right. I am convinced the reason the world is missing global leadership is the same reason America is suffering through a cultural war. America and the world are both missing *courageous leadership*.

Take a moment and re-read the quote from Aikman. Notice his emphasis on the culture wars. He believes the culture cannot be recreated through political decisions alone, but firmly believes:

> It can be changed by the kind of awakening or revival that has such a dramatic effect that the politics is merely an outflow of it . . . the kind of awakening spiritually that this country has seen on at least two previous occasions.[3]

This kind of spiritual revival and cultural reformation will not occur without men in this country stepping forward in a courageous way. I am deeply convinced courage is the greatest need of the hour.

Great leaders emerge in times of major crisis. Hitler emerged as a leader in Germany in desperate times. Churchill, Roosevelt, and eventually Truman emerged in response to a world crisis. The world is ripe today for the emergence of major leaders. I believe the level of world leadership we enjoy is determined by the degree of courage demonstrated.

Courage is one of the reasons Newt Gingrich, speaker of the house of United States Representatives (R-Georgia), is emerging as a decisive leader. His courage to reform and renew America has provided fresh hope. Regardless of how you view Gingrich and his political actions, his courage is what got him where he is. He is perhaps the most powerful man in American politics today.

The growing international moral crisis is begging for courageous leadership. The cultural war which competes for the soul of America is crying for courageous leadership. International difference-makers are few because only a few men are answering the call to stand up and be courageous.

What Is Courage?

One of the top lines of sports clothing in America is *No Fear*. Marketing whizzes place memorable sayings on the front or back of T-shirts that complement this phrase. But is that what courage is? Showing no fear?

I don't think so.

> " Courage is not the absence of fear. Who needs courage to face a toothless enemy? "

Courage is not the absence of fear. Who needs courage to face a toothless enemy? You don't need courage to button your shirt or to tie your shoes. Why not? Because these normally aren't fearful activities. But you do need courage to stand against intense opposition, to risk life and limb for your loved ones or for a cherished principle. Why? Because nobody wants to be spurned or die.

Courage is required only when you must face something fearful. It is necessary only when you must get past your fears to achieve some worthwhile goal. Courageous men are not fearless men; fearless men may simply be stupid. Courageous men are those who face down their fears and triumph despite them.

Courage instills confidence in a person regardless of what he might be facing. A person without courage cannot be an encourager. This is one of the reasons so many people today are so discouraged; few courageous people exist to encourage them. As a spiritual champion, God calls you to be courageous. As you increase your courage, you will be increasingly able to encourage other men.

> A person without courage cannot be an encourager. This is one of the reasons so many people today are so discouraged; few courageous people exist to encourage them.

So let me ask you: Are you a man of courage? Do you need a revival of courage in your life? Do you face down difficulty or danger despite fear? Are you known as a timid man or a courageous man?

A courageous man knows that only Jesus Christ can enable him to face his fears and equip him to be a real man of courage. He realizes that through Christ he can face anything. And he remembers that the degree of his courage will determine how much God uses him in the present crises of our day.

Courageous spiritual champions stand tall above others. God can trust them with anything and through everything. Courage is much more than a logo on a designer series. And never was it more needed than today. This chapter will call for the real men to stand up!

Where Are All the Courageous Men?

One of the most courageous men of the Bible was a man named Daniel. He was a man of God who lived as a captive in a place called Babylon. Babylon was the commercial center of the world. Babylon did not worship the one true God, but worshiped many gods. It was a very sensual and pagan place.

Daniel was a consecrated Jew. He worshiped the one true God, Yahweh. He was not filled with compromise like most of the other captives. Daniel stood for what he believed, even when he stood alone. As he faced the difficulties of loving and serving Yahweh God in this sensual and pagan culture, he did so with courage. Daniel's courage is what God used to distinguish him as a great leader in Babylon. There were times when he himself said he was "terrified," but his love for and commitment to God enabled him to move past his fears to spiritual victory.[4]

What was the one quality that set Daniel apart from the other Jews? Courage. Listen, courage has always set one man apart from the masses. Spiritual champions must be men of courage if God is going to use them in a significant way.

Many observations about courage could be made from the life of Daniel, but let's note a number of the ways in which Daniel demonstrated his courage in the midst of the pagan culture that surrounded him. The similarities between Babylon and America are many; therefore, lessons from Daniel's life are very applicable to our own.

Determine in your heart: "I will follow God."

The king of Babylon offered his choice food to Daniel. That may seem insignificant to us, but not to Daniel. The food offered to him was defiled according to Jewish law and was not to be eaten. The wine offered to him had been toasted to the gods of Babylon while the meat had been offered to a pagan god. If Daniel ate or drank, he would have been forced to compromise his spiritual convictions.

Daniel determined he would follow only his God. He would not defile himself. Even though many other Jews were compromising their convictions by eating and drinking, Daniel did not. He submissively sought permission from Ashpenaz to refrain from eating and drinking the king's food in order not to defile himself. This decision could have cost Daniel his life. Yet, he lived by his spiritual convictions and determined he would follow only his God.

As a courageous spiritual champion, you must determine in your heart, "I will follow God." If you make this commitment before the choice is offered to you, you will be more likely to adhere to your conviction. Will you choose to follow God or will you choose to defile yourself? Men living on the brink of the twenty-first century are offered numerous opportunities to compromise their spiritual convictions.

Courageous spiritual champions are willing to stand, even if they have to stand alone. It takes more courage to say "no" to the pressures of our godless culture than to say "yes" to them. Standing with courage will ignite a spirit of courage in others. Daniel's courage became contagious as three other young Jews joined him in his stand. Will you be a twenty-first century Daniel?

Depend on the Lord for an alternate plan.

Daniel offered to Ashpenaz an alternate plan. He asked Ashpenaz to supply him and his friends with vegetables and water for ten days. At the end of this period, he asked Ashpenaz to compare the health of these four courageous Jews with the rest of the people. Intrigued with the courage of Daniel, Ashpenaz took the challenge. At the end of the ten days, the four men appeared more healthy than all the others, so they were allowed to continue eating vegetables and drinking water. This would permit them to honor God by not defiling their bodies.

God gave Daniel an alternate plan. God is merciful and gracious to a courageous man. Daniel was confident that God had another plan since he knew God would not want him to defile his body with food and drink offered to pagan gods.

When you are faced with a critical decision about whether to cave in to compromise or stand strong with courage, ask God to show you His alternative. I believe God will give it to men who want to honor Him.

The challenge every spiritual leader has in his home is to provide spiritual alternatives for his children when they are tempted to compromise their spiritual convictions. Just saying "no" is not good enough. They need to be given an alternative. Whether it involves plans on prom night or after a game, a positive alternative needs to be offered. Young people are far more likely to compromise their spiritual convictions when they are not given a creative and godly alternative to that which dishonors God.

> **When you are faced with a critical decision about whether to cave in to compromise or stand strong with courage, ask God to show you His alternative.**

A Christian alternative is not compromise. It is God's way of rewarding us for standing with courage. He gave such a plan to Daniel. He will give one to you when you need it. God rewards men of courage.

Develop a conviction: "When I honor God, I know He will honor me."

Daniel was a man of great conviction. He never considered compromise. He knew that when he honored God, the Lord his God would honor him. The Bible says in Daniel 1:9, "Now God granted Daniel favor and compassion in the sight of the commander of the officials."

Why did God do this? Because Daniel had demonstrated courage by sticking to his spiritual convictions. He could have compromised, but he didn't.

First Samuel 2:30 speaks to this subject. It says, "Those who honor me I will honor." When we honor God, He will honor us. He will never let us down if we will stand for Him courageously.

God honored Daniel in the presence of Ashpenaz, his authority. God also honored the four Jews with insight and wisdom. He gave Daniel the ability to understand visions and dreams. In fact, God elevated Daniel and his three Jewish friends beyond their wildest dreams. God honored Daniel and his friends because they honored Him.

God is still looking for men who will honor Him. Will you be like Daniel? The world is crying out for some twenty-first-century Daniels.

Declare God's message to others.

God continued to bless Daniel with great insight and understanding. When others could not interpret the dreams of the king, Daniel could. Daniel was a man for all seasons—even the season of turmoil and misunderstanding.

Years passed and Daniel was brought before king Belshazzar to interpret some disturbing graffiti which had been written on the wall by God Himself. The king offered wealth and position to Daniel if he would interpret the writing, but Daniel, the pure man of God, let him know quickly he was not for sale. He told Belshazzar he would interpret the writing, but not for money. Daniel boldly declared how God had brought down the previous king, Nebuchadnezzar, because of his pride and arrogance. Belshazzar knew this, yet he had exalted himself against God, and that is why God had written on the wall. Daniel declared that Babylon would die as a nation. Belshazzar's face became pale and his knees weak as Daniel pronounced the death of his nation.

Before that very evening had passed, Belshazzar was killed and Babylon was crushed. Darius the Mede became the new ruler of Babylon.

Is God telling you anything about our nation? Will you as a businessman, a churchman, a Christian man have the courage to declare God's message regardless of what it is? God may not reveal His message to you if you don't have the courage to declare it to others.

Without a spiritual revival in this country, the handwriting is on the wall for America. God's judgment will be fierce. America is no different from Babylon in the day of Daniel. America is defaming God and exalting herself, unmindful of His statutes.

Twenty-first-century Daniels are needed to trumpet the message of repentance and revival. All spiritual champions must join in sharing this message. We must declare boldly the truth of God.

If you were invited into the presence of our president and he asked for your evaluation of where America stands morally and spiritually, what would you say? Would you tell him the truth? Or would you seek his approval by telling him that he is on the right path and that things are looking good?

Daniel did not try to create a "win-win" for everyone in Babylon. He told the truth. Truth often results in a "win-lose" situation. Compromising Christians are not major players in the kingdom of God, but Christians who have courage and convictions can make a revolutionary difference in their culture.

We need spiritual champions who will declare God's message in their families, communities, schools, churches, and in the political process. America will go down unless spiritual champions begin to stand up. Will you stand? Will you stand courageously? Will you stand alone?

The time is now to declare the message of God. Whatever your sphere of influence in life, use it courageously for Christ. The Lord will use men of courage.

How to Be Used of God

A man's courage determines how much God will use him. Courageous men are used by God to make a difference.

One of the most courageous men I know is Dr. Adrian Rogers, senior pastor of the Bellevue Baptist Church in Memphis, Tennessee. When God called him to preach and was grooming him in those early years, He blessed him with a great measure of courage. Dr. Rogers preaches with tremendous boldness as hundreds of thousands watch him on television weekly. As a leader in his denomination, he has offered fearless leadership, always standing strong on the inerrancy of Scripture, regardless of the consequences. Due to his fearless leadership, the denomination he loves stands strong as a major influence in Christianity today. Having courage has never damaged Dr.

Rogers or his ministry potential. In fact, his courage has determined the places and the ways God has used him.

How does God want to use you as a spiritual champion? As your courage is strengthened, will you make yourself available to be used of God? As a courageous spiritual champion, you can be used of God to . . .

Lead your family in godliness.

It takes courage to lead a family toward God. It takes courage for a family to follow the ways of godliness rather than the ways of the world. Going with God means you will be going against this world. As this tension increases, the temptation will be to compromise. Do not compromise. Go on with God.

As the spiritual leader of your family, have the courage to go on with God. Lift His standard high in your family. Your leadership under God is not up for a vote. You are not trying to win a popularity contest. You are to lift up the standard of God so that His ways are seen clearly and followed specifically.

I am continually challenged in my role as a father. Being a father is the greatest joy of my life, but it is not easy. Pastoring a large church is an easier task, at times, than that of fathering.

I have often sat down with my boys and challenged them in the area of sexual purity. I hold the line tight in regard to the movies they see. I am responsible for Josh and Nick. I warn them of sensuality and hold them accountable in this area. I ask them periodically about their quiet times with God. As young boys they were taught this discipline and have continued it with honorable consistency.

Courageous spiritual champions lead their families in godliness. They are not bent toward compromise. They raise high the standard of God in the home. First, for themselves and their walk with Christ. Second, for the rest of their families. Godliness is more caught than taught. Let your family catch godliness from your leadership.

Speak God's truth to others.

As a courageous spiritual champion you will be available to God to speak His truth to other people. As you are filled with holy boldness, God will use you to speak to others. To the degree you are filled with courage, you will be used of God to make a difference.

As a spiritual champion, you are called to speak God's truth to men and women who do not yet know Jesus Christ personally. Never back away from declaring a positive word about Jesus Christ. Declare boldly that Jesus is the only way to God. Develop relationships with people who

> " Never back away from declaring a positive word about Jesus Christ. Whenever God opens the door, speak God's truth with courage. "

do not know Christ so that you may be able to witness to them. Whenever God opens the door, speak God's truth with courage.

Speak God's truth to Christians who are not right with Him. Hold the standard of God high among your Christian brothers and sisters. Do not compromise in any way. They need to hear the truth. If they are considering divorce, they need to be told that God says divorce is wrong. If they are in conflict with a Christian friend, call them to uphold God's standard of harmony in the body of Christ. If they are living in open disobedience to God in any area, remind them of what God expects of them. Wouldn't you want someone to have the courage to do this for you?

Turn America back to God.

Just as God used one man named Daniel in a major way in the life of his nation, he can use you. He wants you to make a difference in America. Courageous spiritual champions can make a difference in America.

We men need to become so concerned for America that we do whatever it takes to turn America back to God. We need to pray, fast, and repent so that God's power will once again be outpoured on this nation. This is the greatest way we can be used of God to turn America back to Him.

Beyond this, many of us need to become involved in the political process of this nation. We need to exercise the right to vote. We need the courage to call both political parties and political independents to become pro-family and pro-morality. Why not consider becoming a candidate for public office? Courageous spiritual champions could change communities by becoming school board members or city councilmen. Others could be elected as state legislators. Some may consider running for a national office. Remember, courage is contagious. People are drawn to men who will demonstrate courageous leadership.

These are just some of the ways God may use you to turn our nation back to God. Never discount the power of what one man can do. Daniel was just one man, yet God used him to influence his nation. You are just one man. Pray for courage, that God may raise you to a level of spiritual influence beyond anything you have ever imagined. God's favor comes to the men who honor him. Especially to men of courage.

It's Time

Spiritual champions are men of courage. Men who have faced their fears and have accomplished great things despite them. Men who are unwilling to back down from any crisis in their personal lives or in their nation.

In 1994, I preached a message on the life of Daniel. Afterward a young girl in our fellowship named Makisa Upton wrote the following poem on Daniel 1:1-7 and sent it to me. The poem is titled, "It's Time."

It's time to take a stand,
save your home and land.

Although you're only one,
the battle has been won.
Stand for faith and truth today,
to this world show the way.
In everything you go through,
for God alone stand true.
Though the world has much to give,
for the Lord only I'll live.
Making known God's only way,
living in purity and honor each day.

It's time for twenty-first-century Daniels to stand with courage in our families, in our schools, in our communities, in our political process, in our churches, and in our country. Stand with courage and God will stand with you.

1. How would you define courage? When does someone need it?

2. Would you consider yourself a man of courage? Explain.

3. Ronnie writes, "Courage has always set one man apart from the masses. Spiritual champions must be men of courage if God is going to use them in a significant way." What does he mean, and do you agree with him? Why or why not?

4. What does Ronnie say a spiritual champion must determine in his heart? How can he carry out this determination?

5. What kind of "alternate plans" has God given you when you found yourself in a sticky situation? Describe one of them.

6. Read 1 Samuel 2:30. What tremendous promise is given here? How can it transform the way we respond to threatening situations?

7. What do you think is the message God wants you to declare to others? Do you find this easy to declare? Explain.

8. How do you lead your family toward dependence on God. What specific things do you do?

9. America is a big country. What can you do in your sphere of influence to "turn America back to God"? What could you do that you haven't as yet done? What keeps you from doing these things? What would it take to move you more in the right direction?

10. Who is the most spiritually courageous person you know personally? What made him or her so courageous? What can you learn from this person?

CHAPTER TWELVE

The Legacy of a
Spiritual Champion

A legacy is something of great value that has been handed down from the past. I consider the legacy passed on to me to be tremendously blessed. Many people from varied backgrounds have contributed so much to my life, some directly and others indirectly. I am a product of a wonderful legacy created by people I regard as spiritual champions. As I describe the legacy handed down to me, I hope that you can recall your own legacy and be grateful as for it as I am for my own.

A Blessed Legacy

My father and mother, John and Elva, are both spiritual champions. They have injected into my life so many positive convictions. I received my tenacity from my father who will not let anything or any project go until it is completed. As a door-to-door salesman, Dad's tenacity was a necessity if the family's needs were to be met.

My dad also taught me one of the major tenets of leadership. He taught me the importance of follow-through. I'm not sure he knew he was doing this, but if an assignment was given to me, he held me accountable to complete it.

My mom was the standard-bearer in the home. She reminded the entire family of our responsibility to God. Mom was converted in an evangelistic crusade held in the early 1960s by the prominent evangelist Freddie Gage. Her life was changed from being religious to being spiritual. As she grew in the faith, she held the standard high in the home. My prophetic nature was passed on to me from my mother.

In our family, church took center stage. This spiritual legacy is a torch that will never stop burning in my heart. The small church of some forty people in which I was raised became part of my parents' efforts to instill in me the conviction that the Bible was the inspired Word of God. There was no room for compromise concerning God's Word. Commitment to Christ and His church were imperative. The optional and convenient mentality of our day would have been considered heresy when I was growing up.

One day, if Jesus tarries and I must face the trauma of burying my mother and father, my heart will surge with gratitude for the legacy they have given to me. I have received the mantle from each of them and will pass it on to my children and grandchildren accordingly.

My enthusiasm for Jesus was a legacy given to me by Mike Shillings. Mike was the nineteen-year-old pastor of my church when I was a teenager. He was very influential in my life-changing conversion to Jesus Christ. He demonstrated that Jesus Christ was someone worth being fired up about. Even though Mike is only a few years older than I, God used his enthusiasm for Jesus Christ to influence me greatly.

Upon my call to preach, a dynamic businessman-turned-evangelist made a major mark on my life. As he was storming through Southwest Texas with his compelling challenge to be empowered by the Holy Spirit, I was drawn to the God this man preached. Honestly, I had never met a Christian like him. His name was Jim Standridge. He was owned only by Jesus Christ—a Jesus man, a radical. Just like the followers of Jesus in the Master's day.

I had lost touch with this brother in the faith until God brought him back into my life a couple of years ago. The journey of brokenness on which God had taken him has provided much encouragement to me. God raised him up to minister to me weekly during my recent forty-day journey in prayer and fasting. Jim is the John the Baptist in my life. He may be unknown to the masses, but he is special to God as a prophet who ministers to other prophets.

In my college years, the teachings of two widely-known men of God were woven into my spiritual legacy. These men, Manley Beasley and Jack Taylor, prompted me to become a "spiritual tapeworm." I would listen to tapes of these two great men of God continually. They imparted to me the dynamic truth that Jesus Christ lived in me. They taught me how to have faith and how to walk with God. They placed upon me the burden of spiritual revival that I still carry today. Even though I have spent very little time with each of these men, their life message still lives in me today.

I had little academic heritage. I was the first in my family to attend college and God had a man waiting for me at Howard Payne University. He looked like a general in the military with his no-nonsense crew cut. He held the line tight in the classroom. James Shields injected in me a desire to pursue critical study of the things of God. Dr. Shields made a statement I will never forget when I asked him about attending seminary. He said, "The sharper the ax, the bigger the blow." His life and words motivated me to pursue and receive my seminary degrees.

While in seminary, the Lord influenced me greatly by the lives of Oscar Thompson and Roy Fish. Both were evangelism professors. Their passion for Jesus and the Great Commission is why I am such a believer in evangelism today. In the dry land of seminary years, the classes of these men offered a welcome spiritual oasis. They taught me not so much with lectures as by their lives.

As a small church pastor in my seminary days, a pastor of a very large church in Austin, Texas, agreed to spend five days in my church. At that time, his was the fastest growing church in all of Texas. This strong leader has been a great encourager to me through the years. Harold O'Chester taught me the basics of building a church. This legacy of church growth has dominated much of my ministry. It always comes back to the basics. Harold taught me those basics.

He and his godly wife, Barbara, have also been models for family life for Jeana and me. They have made us accountable in our commitment to family life. They are real people. Godly people. People who live what they preach. As I have watched them walk through the Refiner's fire, the purity of God is still alive in them.

In those formative years of pastoring, as well as in recent years, many men have stamped the eternal mark of God upon my life. Jimmy Draper has taught me the importance of loving people unconditionally. John Bisagno has often inspired me as I have heard him preach at a Texas Baptist Evangelism Conference. Ed Young has made an imprint on my life and ministry by giving me the desire to see God enlarge the kingdom of God through me. The wisdom and courage of Adrian Rogers will invigorate me until I die. The spiritual balance of this man of God sets my soul aflame with the goal of being all God wants me to be.

Legacy. It is something of great value handed down from the past. Pages, even volumes, could be written about these and others whom God has used to make me who I am today.

In these moments of reflection, I am reminded that God uses people. He has placed the right person in my life at the right time to teach me just what I needed to know. Sometimes He uses people in our lives and they do not even know it. As He constructs His workmanship—you and me—He does so in unique ways in each of us.

The people I have mentioned in this chapter are all spiritual champions. Spiritual champions are difference-makers. These people have made a monumental difference in my life. They have passed on to me a burning torch that I will, in turn, pass to others.

Passing the Torch

Not all spiritual champions have received a spiritual legacy, but all spiritual champions leave a legacy. They are not islands to themselves, but reach out and touch others. As they live out who they are in Christ, they inspire others with their life

> **Not all spiritual champions have received a spiritual legacy, but all spiritual champions leave a legacy.**

message and passion. Spiritual champions invest in the future, even into future generations.

God's spiritual champions always leave a legacy to other generations. The Bible says in Psalm 79:13, "So we Thy people and the sheep of Thy pasture will give thanks to Thee forever; To all generations we will tell of Thy praise."

The lives of spiritual champions tell all generations about God. They declare His greatness, giving Him praise for all He has done for us.

> **Spiritual champions who live in America are blessed with a dynamic legacy that cannot be forgotten or ignored.**

Even as we should not forget the legacy given to us personally, we should not forget the legacy passed on to us as Americans. Spiritual champions who live in America are blessed with a dynamic legacy that cannot be forgotten or ignored. Spiritual champions are used by God to make a difference in their nation. They are not silent Americans or sideline Americans. They are difference-makers in our nation because they refuse to ignore its history. They consider its historical greatness a compelling force to make a difference in future generations.

The American Legacy

One of the great treasures of every American is the flag of the United States. Whenever this flag is paraded before us we need to understand its symbolism and power.

On June 14, 1777, Congress determined the design of the American flag. Yet it was not until September 3, 1777, that it was announced to the American people.

Red, white, and blue, the colors of the flag, were interpreted by the Continental Congress to mean the following: "White signifies Purity and Innocence; Red, Hardiness and Valor; Blue signifies Vigilance, Perseverance and Justice."[1]

This flag, often known as "Old Glory" or the "Red, White, and Blue," symbolizes many wonderful things.

When we see our flag, it is common to pledge allegiance to our country. This pledge is an oath of loyalty not simply to the flag, but to the nation it represents. The idea for the pledge originated with one of the publishers of a magazine for girls and boys called *The Youth Companions*. Francis Bellamy, a member of the magazine's staff, is given credit for writing the pledge.

President Benjamin Harrison proclaimed the first use of the original pledge on October 12, 1892, during Columbus Day observances in the public schools. The pledge said: "I pledge allegiance to my flag and to the republic for which it stands: one nation, indivisible, with liberty and justice for all."[2]

The words, "my flag," were later changed to "the flag of the United States of America." This amendment was adopted on Flag Day, June 14, 1924.

In 1954, the Congress of the United States jointly amended the pledge with the words, "under God." President Dwight David Eisenhower, upon the adoption of this amendment to the pledge, stated this reaffirmed: "The transcendence of religious faith in America's heritage and future."[3]

On June 14, 1954, Flag Day, the following Pledge of Allegiance was recited from the steps of the Capitol in Washington D.C.: "I pledge allegiance to the flag of the United States of America and to the republic for which it stands: one nation, under God, indivisible, with liberty and justice for all."

This Pledge of Allegiance to our nation's flag is a part of the American legacy left to us.

As I reviewed this history and reflected on today's political climate, I thought how refreshing it would be for our Congress to jointly agree on something—anything, especially acknowledging God in America once more. I also thought how wonderful it would be for our nation's president to acknowledge unashamedly the deep Christian faith rooted in our nation's past, and to be committed that this legacy will continue in the future. It is hard to believe that within a decade of the adoption of the words, "under God," into our pledge of allegiance, we ceased prayer and Bible reading in our public schools. Within a historically short period of time, our nation lurched from adopting an amendment to interject "under God" in the pledge of allegiance to making some of the most detrimental decisions in her history.

> It is hard to believe that within a decade of the adoption of the words, "under God," into our pledge of allegiance, we ceased prayer and Bible reading in our public schools.

As we consider the American legacy passed to us, consider the Pledge of Allegiance to the Flag. This flag symbolizes all we are to stand for as a nation. If our children, grandchildren, and great-grandchildren are going to live in a free nation, then we must pass on to them the truth of our nation's heritage. I believe the Pledge of Allegiance is a good tool which can be implemented to pass on this legacy. Let's focus on several key words in this pledge.

"Allegiance"

The word "allegiance" is both a missing term and practice in American culture today. Allegiance means loyalty, but a lack of allegiance to the flag and to the nation which it represents has grown commonplace. One of the worst examples of this has been the public burning and desecration of the flag. This despicable practice should not be accepted in our country. It is an offense to every true American, but especially those who have died that we might live in a free nation.

America is by no means a perfect country, but we should remain loyal to it in order to make it into the nation God wants it to be. We should do everything we can to see her return to her heritage. We should not allow the insincerity and shallowness of much of our present culture to discolor the deep, genuine loyalty that is due our country. Being an American is a privilege. The more I travel internationally, the more I am grateful to God for allowing me live here. Loyalty to our nation is a part of the great American legacy given to us.

"People"

America is a republic. As a republic, the supreme power rests in the body of our citizens who are empowered to vote. This voting process also gives us representatives who are to make decisions on our behalf about the direction of this country.

The government of America is not located in Washington, D.C., but in every town, village, community, and city in the nation. The government of America is the people of America. The way this nation is governed is determined by the people.

The flag of our nation stands for its people. People from every walk of life. People from the past and people who are living today. America exists as a nation because of the emphasis placed on its citizenry. We are a republic, a nation where the power lies with her people. This is a precious part of our legacy as a nation.

"One Nation"

One of the secrets of our success as a nation is that we are united—one nation. Even though our country is made up of diverse peoples, this diversity has never been a point of weakness but has historically been one of our greatest strengths.

Racial, ethnic, and cultural tensions should cease when speaking of America as one nation. We must always keep the priority of the American agenda. We are to be one nation. Not many, but one nation.

The American legacy passed to us is the knowledge that strength exists because we are united. Even though there are fifty unique states, we are one nation. Regardless of various backgrounds and all kinds of diversity, America must always remember it is one nation.

"God"

Isn't it amazing that the words "under God" were added to the Pledge of Allegiance to the American Flag in 1954? I find it interesting that this phrase was not part of the original pledge. Yet less than one decade later after adding "under God," the Supreme Court ruled to eliminate references to God from public school classrooms. This dreadful decision has brought devastation to our country spiritually, morally, and even academically. It has resulted in prejudice against conservatives who believe that God has a major part in our history. The liberal media has blasted anyone who holds conservative views on the family, morality, and spiritual matters as being "right wing," "extremist," and dangerous.

It is time that many of our politicians go back to school on the history of this nation. America has always been a nation under God. The educational system of this country needs to be held accountable for not telling the entire story concerning our nation's history and the place God has

> "It is time that many of our politicians go back to school on the history of this nation. America has always been a nation under God."

in it. The Americans of the past have left our generation with a legacy concerning God. Now is the time for God to be placed back in America.

"Liberty and Justice"

A high price has been paid in our country for liberty and justice. Any person who does not want to participate in religious practice in a public setting should be given that right. But if a conservative Christian in this country wants to practice his Christianity in a public way, he should also have that right.

Liberty is not the right to do what you *want*; liberty is the right to do what you *ought*. Liberty does not exist outside the necessary parameters, such as the law of the land. When a citizen goes outside the law, justice needs to prevail.

Justice should be meted out fairly to every person. A functional justice system is essential in every setting in America. Men and women have given their lives for the right of every citizen to be treated fairly. The legacy left to us includes a climate in which every citizen of this nation can expect to receive both liberty and justice.

If the American legacy is going to be passed on to future generations of Americans, then concerned citizens must take the needed steps to involve themselves in the political process. For Americans who are family-driven, morally conscious, and value-centered conservatives, it is time for the 175,000 political precincts in this nation to hear from us.

There is no need to be mean or extreme. There is a need to learn about how the political system in this nation works. Since we are a republic, the power lies with the people as they exercise the right to vote. We should always exercise this privilege. Sitting on the bench is unacceptable. It is past time to get involved in the future of America.

What Kind of Legacy Are You Going to Leave?

As I have reviewed the legacy left to us in America, I hope you have begun to consider what kind of personal legacy you are going to leave to others. What kind of legacy are you going to leave to your family, friends, church, school, business place, and nation? May I suggest you consider the following four legacies as a worthy heritage for future generations?

Spiritual Legacy

What kind of spiritual legacy are you leaving the people who know you

> **What kind of legacy are you going to leave to your family, friends, church, school, business place, and nation?**

and the others who may be watching you from a distance? When they think of Jesus Christ, do they think of you? If you were accused of being a follower of Jesus and the people who know you made up the jury, would there be enough evidence to convict you? It is time for us all to sense the urgency to leave a spiritual legacy to others.

Spiritual champions leave a spiritual legacy to future generations. It will not be an abstract concept, but a clear, authentic and genuine heritage. It will be compelling and contagious to future generations.

Spiritual champions leave a spiritual legacy that is Christ-centered, Spirit-powered, ministry-driven, and world-conscious. This is the godly heritage we are called to leave to the people who follow us in this world. If the torch we hand off to the next generation is a weak, flickering spark, it will probably be soon extinguished. Let's light the fire of the next generation with a dynamic spiritual legacy. This is real, spiritual championship living.

Family Legacy

What kind of family legacy are you going to leave the people who know you and who will outlive you? Have you considered what you are conveying to others about the family through your life? Our life never lies. Look at yours. Take a long look and evaluate your commitment to your family.

A spiritual champion is a one-woman man. He remains faithful to his marriage vows. He has made a promise to his spouse and to God, and he keeps his promise. He is a man who spends time with his children. He does not miss the important things in the lives of his children. He begins with the family calendar, rather than the business calendar. A spiritual champion does not sacrifice his family on the altar of a successful career. He knows that would pass on a destructive legacy to his children which will ultimately decimate his family.

Be a man who fulfills your role in family leadership. Be the spiritual leader of your home. Leave the kind of legacy to your family that enables your children and grandchildren to say of you, "My Dad always loved me. The things that were important to me, were important to him."

Moral Legacy

What kind of moral legacy are you leaving your family, friends, and business associates? Are you the kind of man who has a reputation for keeping his word, has a happy wife at home, and lives above board morally?

Spiritual champions play by the rules found in the Word of God. They have no desire to make up new ones or live on the edge of those that exist. Spiritual champions have pure morals.

Take the high road of morality. Stand for it. When you do, you will stand with God. No one loses when he stands with God.

American Legacy

What kind of American legacy are you leaving to your fellow countrymen? How are you responding to the challenges facing our country today?

We need to pass on a legacy of loyalty to this nation. The kind of legacy that reminds people they are the government. The kind of legacy that permits diversity, liberty, and justice for all. We need to leave the kind of legacy that insists that God has had in the past and should have in the future a major part to play in this country.

Take the Challenge

Do you want God to use you as a spiritual champion? He will if you will seize the opportunity to leave a great legacy to those who come after you. Spiritual champions cannot fail to leave a spiritual, family, moral, and strong national legacy to the future generations of this country.

Men, it is time to take the challenge and fan the flame of the torch. Great opportunities abound for each of us who desire to be spiritual champions. Can we do anything less than make a commitment to leave a spiritual, family, moral, and American legacy to others? The people who have shaped our lives have been difference-makers. Let's make a positive difference for future generations with the days God gives us.

S T U D Y   Q U E S T I O N S

1. Do you consider yourself to have received a family legacy? Explain.

2. Who has had the biggest impact on your life in each of the following areas, and why?

A. Academic life

B. Spiritual life

C. Family life

D. Church life

3. What kind of spiritual legacy do you think are you leaving to your own family? Are you satisfied with this legacy? Explain.

4. What is most precious to you about the American legacy? Why?

5. To what persons or institutions or ideas do you give your allegiance? Why?

6. What do the words "liberty" and "justice" convey to you? In what ways does America fulfill these ideas, and in what ways does it seem to fall short?

7. Describe what, in your opinion, would make up the ultimate spiritual legacy. In your own experience, who has come the closest to achieving this ultimate spiritual legacy? Describe him or her.

8. What kind of family legacy do you think you are leaving for your children? What will they remember most about their own growing up years? You might even consider asking them this question.

9. When your children watch the way you operate and the decisions you make, what moral legacy do you think they see? What kind of example are you setting right now?

10. Thinking as realistically as you can, name three things you would like to leave to the American legacy. Why these three things? How can you actually leave them?

CHAPTER THIRTEEN

The Ongoing Challenge of a Spiritual Champion

Over the past three years I have felt compelled to begin investing my energy in the lives of men who have surrendered to serve in full-time ministry. I became convinced that this time would be blessed by the Lord as I made this eternal investment.

The Servant's Fellowship

With this in mind I formed a ministry in our church called, "The Servant's Fellowship." The only way one can become a part of this fellowship is to commit to full-time Christian ministry or be the spouse of one who has made this kind of commitment. Our goal is to meet monthly, with the exception of the summer months. Fifteen to thirty people attend a typical meeting. The number fluctuates because many participants move into other ministries or leave to continue their education.

Our time is unstructured. Formal presentations are rare. Before a semester begins, I survey the group to ask what they would most like to talk about in the coming months. I try to determine what is foremost on their hearts and make it a priority. Two crucial subjects are always discussed. First, the necessity of an ongoing personal walk with Jesus Christ. Second, the struggle in determining the best place of education to be equipped for ministry. We pray for one another as together we face these and other issues.

I have discovered that this time spent investing in the eternity of other people will affect the future of those to whom God calls them. As pastor, I mentor these freshly-called men and women to sense the need for personal accountability. I believe this regular investment of one to one and a half hours could be the best investment I'll ever make.

I have also discovered that as these people come together in a small group with other God-called men and women, it builds fellowship. They enjoy a sense of family as they discover each has been called by God out of the same church. Many times they pray together in and outside the group, which further builds their commitment to God and to one another.

Outside the fellowship, I provide them the opportunity to see me about anything. They are often concerned about the specifics of God's calling and where they ought to go to school. I have never sensed that I've wasted my time when it's been spent with these young men and women. Only the Lord knows how He will one day use these brothers and sisters to serve Him across the world. I enjoy their fellowship immensely.

Before they leave our fellowship to minister or to continue their education, I ask our church to pray for them. The saints who know them and love them, along with our pastors, lay hands on them and pray for them. I talk with the church about our investment in these people over the years and how our ministry will live on through them for generations to come. These prayer times of commitment at the altar have been some of the greatest times in our church. There is much joy and glad weeping.

Two Men Named Brad

Within the last few months, two of these men have left us to continue their education at the Southeastern Baptist Theological Seminary in Wake Forest, North Carolina. Both of these young men have served as interns on our staff, working in our ministry to university students. Both have a hot heart for Jesus. I am confident they will be greatly used of God if they keep their hearts pure before Him. Both are named Brad.

Brad Jurkovich is an outgoing, gregarious guy. He will talk to anyone he meets or sees. Not a trace of timidity inhabits his body. On one occasion recently, he plunged through security in the Atlanta airport to meet and shake the hand of Newt Gingrich, speaker of the House of Representatives in the United States Congress. He has a heart for mass evangelism. He wants to make a major difference in the world for Jesus Christ. His wife, Stephanie, will be a great asset to his ministry.

Brad Graves met Jesus Christ the first time he walked into our church as a senior in high school. God has changed his life radically. His smile and heart capture the attention of Spirit-filled believers. His witness for Jesus is spontaneous. Only days before he left for seminary, I asked him what he was thinking about and dealing with at this time of transition. I will never forget his answer: "Pastor, my prayer every day has been, 'Lord, give me North Carolina for Jesus, or move me back to Arkansas.'" I praise the Lord for this kind of commitment. My heart almost burst with excitement as I reported this conversation with our church. You see, Brad caught it. All the time, money, and effort we spent was a great investment. Priceless!

Mentors for Christ

The ongoing challenge of a spiritual champion is to bring others along in the faith by mentoring them. Spiritual champions have the mandate and the privilege to produce other champions. This will only occur as they invest their lives in other men. The Servants' Fellowship is one way of building spiritual champions for future generations. I want these young men and women to be major players for Jesus Christ as they take the gospel throughout the world.

The need for mentoring is great! I regularly receive telephone calls from across America from men who have questions about their walk with Jesus Christ. Some are laymen who are struggling and have identified with our ministry on television. Others are God-called servants who are in the battle, waging warfare with Satan. They always say, "Pastor Floyd, I just need someone to talk to about this and I wondered if you would take the time for a moment to give me some counsel?" Men are crying out for someone to encourage them in their spiritual lives.

What Does It Mean to Mentor Someone?

Many fine books on mentoring other men are on the market today. My goal in this chapter is to challenge you to understand that each spiritual champion has the responsibility of bringing others along in the faith.

When I speak of mentoring someone in the faith, I am talking about becoming their teacher, guide, coach, counselor, trainer, instructor, and tutor. These are the roles a mentor plays in the lives of other men. The extent of this role may seem overwhelming, but it really isn't. It becomes natural as a spiritual champion simply invests his life in others.

For instance, when I was pastor of the First Baptist Church of Palacios, Texas (a small coastal town between Houston and Corpus Christi), I met a young man named Craig Miller. Craig's mother and father, Wanda and Bert, were stalwart members in the church. On the night I moved to town, I saw Craig at a ball game, holding a can of beer in the school parking lot. I walked up to him and said, "Hello Craig, how are you doing?" You would have thought I had slapped him.

In time, Craig got his life right with God. He was no longer a radical for the devil, but for Jesus. Eventually he felt the call of God and surrendered his life to full-time Christian ministry. After graduating from high school, he attended Howard Payne University and Southwestern Baptist Theological Seminary. He joined my staff as an intern while I was serving in another church. His first full-time ministry position was in Chandler, Arizona. In 1989, he again joined my staff to serve as our minister to university students. Eventually his position expanded to being in charge of evangelism training and our world missions ministry. Feeling a new call on his life, Craig resigned his position in 1995 as he and his wife, Vicky, prepared to enter full-time evangelism and world missions ministry, but he still serves our fellowship in a part-time capacity as our coordinator of world missions ministry. He is a great preacher and Vicky is a gifted singer. Both are anointed by God's Spirit and have the world on their hearts.

I have mentored Craig Miller since the early 1980s. Even though we have not met on a weekly basis for this purpose, I have invested my life in him. I'm convinced this investment will pay great dividends in the expansion of the kingdom of God across the world.

I often have been Craig's teacher. I cannot count the times we have discussed passages of Scripture or spiritual principles. At other times, I have served as his guide as he has moved through various transitions. I have been his coach. I have challenged him and gotten in his face. I also have served as his counselor. There were occasions when he said I was the only person he could trust to share his heart with. When Craig has needed a trainer, I have been that. When he needed someone to instruct him in his faith and in his ministry, I had the privilege of serving as his friendly instructor. When he has struggled in a particular area of his life, I have served as his tutor.

Please don't misunderstand. This is not the "look and see what Ronnie has done for Craig show." The relationship I have had with Craig Miller has been a mentoring relationship, built on love and trust. I have been willing to invest in his life and he has been willing to learn. All mentoring relationships depend on those two things.

One of the most exciting times is when I have seen God use Craig in the lives of others. When he leads others to Jesus Christ I am filled with joy. When God uses him to mentor younger men than himself—many of them surrendering to the ministry—I am ecstatic. His success is a dividend from the investment I have made in his life. It thrills my heart to see how God is raising him up to influence another generation. All praise to Jesus!

> **Mentoring is not an "elite status." It simply requires that one man make an investment of his time in the life of another man.**

Why do I tell you all this? One reason is to dispel the belief that only a few can become mentors to other men. Mentoring is not an "elite status." It simply requires that one man make an investment of his time in the life of another man or the lives of a group of men. It is passing on the torch to another person through the marathon relay of life.

I have heard John MacArthur say on occasion, "To disciple another person, you just have to know a little more than they do about the subject." I love that statement. Mentoring and discipling is not difficult. There is no single way or method of doing it. Mentoring other men simply means one life investing in another. Such a Christ-centered relationship will pay eternal dividends.

How to Maintain a Spiritual Edge

As I grow older, one of my most pressing concerns is that I will be able to stay on the cutting edge. I do not want to become stale spiritually. I do not want to become irrelevant professionally.

I am convinced that mentoring younger men will keep me sharp for Jesus. It will help me to maintain a spiritual and professional edge. A service of Leadership Network called NETFAX had this to say about maintaining such a spiritual edge:

How does a leader maintain a spiritual edge? Many say the best way to stay on the cutting edge is to invest in those who live there. Those who currently live in a crucible [heat-resisting container] have a contagious hunger for change. Those who have overcome their crucible need the constant reminder of the time when they had more to gain than to lose. The informal interchange between the two leaders is sometimes called mentoring.[1]

God takes each of us through some difficult transitions in life. He has not done it for our benefit alone, but for those who will follow us in a similar situation. The spiritual lessons we learn transcend the problems, and in a mentoring relationship they allow us to help others through a similar struggle. We are reminded of the grace God provided when we went through it ourselves.

Maintain a spiritual edge.

One of the ways to maintain a spiritual edge is to invest yourself in someone else. It will keep you sharp. It will challenge you. It will get you outside of yourself and force you to be a giver of your life, time, and heart. Investing your life in others will help you maintain a spiritual edge.

Some of the guys I have mentored throughout the years have asked me questions for which I had no answers. They have held me accountable in my walk with Christ. They have challenged me to think through my faith and the statements of my faith. Mentoring others cannot help but keep you on the spiritual edge for Jesus Christ.

Be willing to mentor others.

God wants to use each spiritual champion to mentor other men. The real meaning of a man becomes clear as you experience the mentoring relationship. Howard and William Hendricks' book, *Iron Sharpens Iron*, says, "In our experience, there are far more men looking for mentors than there are willing to serve as mentors."

The absence of male leadership in the family has accentuated the need for mentoring other men. Role models are missing in the home. Many so-called role models are wasting their opportunities of influence through poor moral and spiritual choices. Spiritual champions need to be willing to mentor other men.

Right now I am praying seriously about how I might be able to mentor other young pastors across this nation. I want to help them and I know it will help me. I believe it will help the expansion of the kingdom of God.

Pray for someone in whom you can invest your life by mentoring them. Keep it simple. Beware of programming it. Allow God to work through you both for your mutual edification and His glory.

Help Others Become Spiritual Champions

I believe if a man gets close to a true spiritual champion, he will become one. At the very least, the probability is increased. Spiritual champions produce spiritual champions. This is why I want to be around men who have a greater walk with God than I do and a greater vision for the world. We become like the people we associate with.

> If a man gets close to a true spiritual champion, he will become one. Spiritual champions produce spiritual champions.

Mentoring is not a new principle. Throughout the Bible, we see the ministry of mentoring. Elijah mentored Elisha. Daniel mentored Shadrach, Meshach, and Abednego. Moses mentored Joshua. Paul mentored Timothy. Barnabas mentored Mark. Jesus mentored his twelve disciples, especially Peter, James, and John.

Jesus spent his public ministry of almost three years investing in the lives of twelve men. He taught them, guided them, coached them, counseled them, trained them, instructed them, and tutored them. This is true mentoring. He invested His life in them. They went where He went. Most of them were teachable, some more than others. Regardless, Jesus loved and accepted them unconditionally—even when He knew one of them would eventually betray Him!

Jesus invested both His time and His life in the twelve disciples. All that Jesus was He placed into them. He injected Himself into their lives. This relationship serves as a model for us to follow today. How can you mentor other men to become spiritual champions?

By Investing Your Time

Time does not belong to you, but to God. It is really His time; however, you are the steward of the time God has given you. You will one day stand before Him and give an account of the time you have spent here on earth.

All of us make time for what is important to us. What gets our attention is our priority. Too many of us invest our time in things that will not matter in eternity. The only things going to heaven are people. Therefore, the only eternal investment any of us can make is in other people.

You can mentor other men in the faith by spending time with them. It may need to be a structured time with an agenda. If you're looking for ideas, you could use this book for your agenda by reading and discussing one chapter per week. The key is time.

Spiritual champions make time for what really matters in life. Spiritual champions make time for other men. They understand that other men need help, encouragement, and strength. Let God use you to build others in the faith.

By Investing Your Life

Your life does not belong to you. You belong to God. I use the second person pronoun "your" only in the sense that God has entrusted life to you. You are responsible and accountable to Him for what you do with it. As the steward of your life, you need to remember that you own nothing, but are responsible to God for everything you do.

What are you going to do with your life? In what are you going to invest it? Men need other men. We need someone besides our family members to share and experience life. Our families are to be our priorities, yet mentoring relationships can help us even to be better family men.

Spiritual champions do not waste their lives in meaningless things. They make use of the time they have on this earth to invest in the lives of other men. By investing in the future of others, you can live on even after your physical death. The life of God that you have injected into other men will stay with them forever.

Fanning into Flame

Men are yearning for someone to be their guide, teacher, and coach. Remember, you must be only one step ahead of them to mentor them. "Knowing it all" is not the issue. No one knows it all but God.

> Men are yearning for someone to be their guide, teacher, and coach. Remember, you must be only one step ahead of them to mentor them.

The exciting move of God that is happening among men today brings many challenges. The Promise Keepers movement is astounding and miraculous, drawing hundreds of thousands of men to major rallies across the country. Men come away energized in their faith like never before. Yet after thrilling to the excitement of being with thousands of other believers in Jesus Christ, they will have to go back to the daily grind of life and there live out their faith. The Jesus they discovered at that rally is the same Jesus who accompanies them to their workplace, yet the challenges before them will be great.

This is why we need one another. We need to fan the flames of what God is doing in this nation and across the world. A mentoring relationship can accomplish this. Spiritual champions build other spiritual champions by investing their time and lives in other men.

What each of us needs today is goose sense. What is goose sense?

Goose Sense, Fact 1: As each goose flaps its wings, it creates an "uplift" for the birds that follow. By flying in "V" formation, the whole flock adds 71 percent greater flying range than if each bird flew alone. *Lesson:* People who share a common direction and sense of community can get where they are going quicker and easier, because they are traveling on the thrust of one another.

Goose Sense, Fact 2: When a goose falls out of formation, it suddenly feels the drag and resistance of flying alone. It quickly moves back into formation to take advantage of the lifting power of the bird immediately in front of it. *Lesson:* If we have as much sense as a goose, we will stay in formation with those headed where we want to go. We are willing to accept their help and give help to others.

Goose Sense, Fact 3: When the lead goose tires, it rotates back into the formation and another goose flies into the point position. *Lesson:* It pays to take turns doing the hard tasks and sharing leadership. As with geese, people are interdependent on each other's skills, capabilities and unique arrangements of gifts, talents or resources.

Goose Sense, Fact 4: The geese flying in formation honk to encourage those in front to keep up their speed. *Lesson:* We need to make sure our honking is encouraging. In groups where there is encouragement the production is greater.

Goose Sense, Fact 5: When a goose gets sick, wounded or shot down, two geese drop out of formation and follow it down to help or protect it. They stay with it until it dies or is able to fly again. Then they launch out with another formation or catch up with the flock. *Lesson:* If we have as much sense as a goose, we will stand by each other in difficult times as well as when we are strong.[2]

Men, it just makes goose sense that mentoring should have a place in each of our lives. No doubt a mentoring relationship can improve your spiritual flying range at least 71 percent. If God made a goose with that much sense, surely His wisdom abounds toward us in an even greater measure.

Will You Answer the Call?

God wants to use you as a spiritual champion. You were designed to be a spiritual champion for the kingdom of God. One of the most potent ways God can use you is in the lives of other men for the purpose of building their faith.

The purpose of mentoring men is to facilitate change in these men so that they can change the world. We cannot change them, but God can, through our lives. The ongoing challenge of a spiritual challenge is to bring others along in the faith. Not only in introducing them to Jesus Christ, but in developing that relationship. As men are changed by the power of Jesus Christ, He will enable them to change the world. This is our hope. This is God's strategy to bring the world into a right relationship with Him.

> " The purpose of mentoring men is to facilitate change in these men so that they can change the world. "

One by one, men come to God.
One by one, men grow in their faith.
One by one, men mentor and are mentored by other men.
One by one, men can change the world.

Spiritual champions are world-changers. They are difference-makers. When you become a spiritual champion, you at last will learn the true meaning of man.

1. When you hear the word "mentoring," what comes to mind? Did anyone mentor you? If so, describe the person.

2. Ronnie quotes John MacArthur as saying, "To disciple another person, you just have to know a little more than they do about the subject." What encouragement is this saying trying to give us?

3. How is it possible to maintain a spiritual edge? What specifically can you do?

4. Are you willing to mentor others? Explain.

5. Howard and William Hendricks write, "In our experience, there are far more men looking for mentors than there are willing to serve as mentors." Why do you think this is true? Would it be true of you? Explain.

6. Ronnie writes, "I believe if a man gets close to a true spiritual champion, he will become one." Why is this so often true? What spiritual champion can you get close to?

7. Becoming a mentor involves investing your time. Where in your schedule could you carve out some time to serve as a mentor. It doesn't have to be a lot of time—where could the time come from?

8. Is there anyone who has invested his life in you? If so, describe what he did. If you had no such person, would you have liked to have had a mentor? If so, who can you mentor?

9. Read through "Goose Sense" at the end of the chapter. What lesson most helped you? What lesson most entertained you? What lesson most surprised you? What lesson do you most want to put into practice.

10. Discuss Ronnie's closing statement: "Spiritual champions are world-changers. They are difference-makers. When you become a spiritual champion, then at last you will learn the true meaning of man." What does he mean? Do you agree with him? Why or why not?

EPILOGUE

The Championship Game

Game day is one of the most exciting times in the world of sports. Teams practice all week preparing for the day of the game. Olympic athletes train their entire lives preparing for the moment of competition. The future of athletes and coaches depends upon their performances at the moment of competition.

Life is not like athletics. In life, every day is game day. There is no such thing as the off season. There is no such thing as practice or dress rehearsal. Each day we play for all the marbles.

In the same way, every day is a championship game for a spiritual champion. This championship game may be in your personal life, family, church, or in the marketplace. At times, you may be playing for everything in each of these areas. Spiritual champions wouldn't think of running away from the challenge of game day, but embrace it in spiritual power.

Contemporary spiritual champions need to be like the men of Hebron referred to in 1 Chronicles 12:38.

> All these, being men of war, who could draw up in battle formation, came to Hebron with a perfect heart, to make David king over all Israel; and all the rest also of Israel were of one mind to make David king.

In the New International Version this same verse says, "All these were fighting men who volunteered to serve in the ranks."

The mighty men of Hebron were fired up. They were ready for the task at hand. Their people lay in spiritual tragedy and they wanted the touch of God again.

Spiritual champions are warriors like the fighting men of Hebron. They train for war. They volunteer to do spiritual battle. These warriors are ready and even hungry for combat. They are aggressive in taking action for God.

While spiritual wimps play games with God and know the "ins and outs" of Religion 101, spiritual warriors have a heart for God and take seriously the challenge before them. These spiritual champions are "difference makers" who desire God to give their families, their churches, their businesses, and their nation a mighty spiritual revival. They play every down of life as though it is a championship game. And it is. Life has no scrimmages.

In this book, you have learned how to win your spiritual championship. I have described how to keep your spiritual championship by having the right priorities and making the right choices. I have warned you not to lose your spiritual championship by coddling "rattlesnakes" in your life. I have challenged you to utilize your spiritual championship to build other spiritual champions for Jesus Christ.

Since you've made it this far, I know you want God to refresh you spiritually. I believe many of you will carry the burden for spiritual revival in our nation, beginning in each of your churches. God is going to bring a mighty spiritual awakening to the remnant in this nation which yearns for God's touch. I believe this revival will transcend all denominational, ethnic, racial, and cultural lines. The remnant of God is waking up! Do not miss it.

It is time for us to run the race of life as spiritual champions. The apostle Paul, one of the great spiritual champions of the past, said: "Run in such a way that you may win." Spiritual champions run to win the race of life. Take the charge. Race like a spiritual champion. Then the prize will be yours.

Remember to take the "8:37 check" and the "4:13 check" continually. Spiritual champions are conquerors who can do all things through Jesus Christ. The way you run in life will reveal what you believe about God and about yourself. Run like the man God says you are. Run like a spiritual champion.

One day you will receive the championship ring called heaven. You will finish the course as a spiritual champion. You will spend all of eternity in worship of Jesus Christ, the Lamb of God.

Before you receive your championship ring, if Jesus does not return first, you will pass through death. As you have the opportunity to look back over your life, you will want to be able to know that you made a difference in your life for Jesus Christ. You want to have your family and friends say, "This man was a spiritual champion, a real man of God."

What they say about you and what you think about yourself will be determined by how you respond to the message of this book. Obedience is the beginning point of spiritual revival. Take what you have read seriously. Implement the principles daily. Become what God has empowered you to be in His Son Jesus Christ. Choose to be a spiritual champion!

Every day is a championship game in the life of a spiritual champion. The real meaning of a man is discovered when he realizes God has provided him with all the resources necessary to become a spiritual champion. Now that you know this, go out and play the game in the power of God's Holy

Spirit. Your family, business, friends, church, and nation hang in the balance. I urge you to answer the call.

N O T E S

Chapter 1

1. *Time*, Vol. 145, No. 18, 1 March 1995, 36.

2. If you have never begun this journey with Jesus Christ, there will never be a better time to do so than now. Pray the following words to God. Mean them in your heart and let Jesus make a difference in you.

> *Dear God,*
> *I know I am a sinner. I know I do wrong every day of my life. I turn from my sins right now and turn toward Jesus. I believe Jesus died for my sins. I believe Jesus was raised from the dead for me. By faith, I receive Jesus Christ into my life right now. I trust only in Jesus for my eternal salvation. I trust only in Jesus to make a difference in me. Thank you for giving me eternal life and changing me. Amen.*

If you sincerely prayed this prayer, the words you just spoke to God far outweigh what any man-made religion could ever do for you. The "Difference-Maker" has just come into your life! *You plus Jesus equals a difference.* Congratulations! You have just taken the first and most important step to becoming a spiritual champion!

Chapter 4

1. Walton, Sam. "Sam Walton Recounts the Life of a Salesman," *Time*, Vol. 139, No. 24, 15 June 1992, page 57.

2. Ibid., 54.

3. Ibid., 53.

4. Jack Welch, "What Sam Walton Taught America," *Fortune*, Vol. 125, No. 9, 4 May 1992, 105.

5. Quoted in John Piper, *Let the Nations Be Glad: The Supremacy of God in Missions* (Grand Rapids, Mich.: Baker Book House, 1993), 12.

6. In my first book, *Reconnecting*, I go into extensive detail about how to have a consistent, quality, daily time with God. I am convinced that our Christian life will never exceed our daily time with God. This is why I gave much greater detail in *Reconnecting* to this subject. It is a book that explains how to personally walk with Christ.

Chapter 5

1. "Focus Fanatic," *Success Magazine*, January-February 1994, 1-5.

2. "All Fired Up," *Time*, Vol. 145, No. 25, 19 June 1995, 20-26.

Chapter 6

1. Rolf Zettersten, *Dr. Dobson: Turning Hearts Toward Home* (Dallas: Word Publishing, 1989), 171.

2. Ibid.

3. God has given me a vision for America. I believe He is going to send a mighty spiritual awakening to the people of God. This movement of God is going to transcend all denominational, cultural, ethnic, and racial lines. The walls are going to come down. The remnant of God across America will answer the call of God for revival. Some will pray, others will pray and fast. As God's people humble themselves, God will accomplish His work of revival.

Brothers, God is already beginning a great move in this country. Many of you have been a part of this spiritual movement. Due to God's sovereign grace and power, our church has begun to experience this awakening. What God began on Sunday, June 4, 1995, He is continuing. Our church will never be the same again.

When God moves spiritually throughout the remnant in America, this country will never be the same. Whatever Jesus touches, He changes. Let's pray and fast with the goal of seeking Jesus to change America. What God is doing in America is bigger than you and me. It is bigger than anything you have ever been a part of in your life. Do not miss it. You can influence America!

Men, God gave me a plan for America. He wants me to make a difference. He has called me to pray and fast for the spiritual condition of this country. This is why I answered His call to fast and pray for forty days for spiritual revival. God has also called me to declare His Word via television throughout this nation. In this recent forty-day fast, He called me to go throughout America and lead what He wants me to call, "Awaken America" rallies. The purpose of these one-night rallies is to call God's people to spiritual revival. I share this plan with you because this is what God has called me to do. He will determine the dimension of each of these things, as well as their success.

Chapter 8

1. "What Makes Olympic Athletes?" *The Reader's Digest*, Vol. 144, No. 862, February 1992, 117-120.

2. Ibid., 117.

Chapter 10

1. These three Nazarite vows can be found in Numbers 6:1-8.

Chapter 11

1. David Aikman, "Christian Philosophy, Amerioca and the World," *Net-Fax*, Number 6, Nov. 14, 1994.

2. Ibid.

3. Ibid.

4. See Daniel 4:19; 7:7,19,28; 8:17. Also see Daniel 10:12,19.

Chapter 12

1. *Funk & Wagnall's Standard Reference Encyclopedia*, Vol. 10 (New York: Standard Reference Works Publishing Co., 1961), 3532.

2. Ibid., 3530.

3. Ibid., 3533.

Chapter 13

1. "Mentoring on Both Sides of the Equation," *NetFax*, No. 22, 26 June 1995.

2. Angela Arrison, "Goose Sense," *Professional Women's Newsletter*, Vol. 1, No. 4, July 1995.

"In a day when men are being called to take back their God-given role and responsibility, Ronnie Floyd has given eminently practical advice on how to be 'God's man.' If you want to be a spiritual champion, read this book."

DAVID "MAC" MCQUISTON, FOCUS ON THE FAMILY

"I heartily commend Dr. Floyd's important emphasis on true, biblical masculinity. There are few things more needed in every area of American life than a rediscovery of godly masculinity. Dr. Floyd's book is an essential tool in helping people in this discovery."

DR. RICHARD LAND, PRESIDENT, CHRISTIAN LIFE COMMISSION, NASHVILLE, TENNESSEE

"Finally, a manual on how to be a champion in the most important arenas of our life. This stuff works! I have found these principles will make a champion out of you from the locker room to the board room to your family room. Dr. Ronnie Floyd has shown us that it's never too late to be the person you want to be."

DR. JAY H. STRACK, FOUNDER, JAY STRACK ASSOCIATION

"In terms we all can understand, Ronnie Floyd challenges us to be the men God intended. If ever our world needed manly spiritual champions, it is now!"

DR. ROBERT LEWIS, PASTOR, FELLOWSHIP BIBLE CHURCH, LITTLE ROCK, ARKANSAS

"This book has reminded me about what really is important. You will be challenged to be a difference maker, both at home and at work. It has been like a wake-up call to me."

ROCKEY FELKER, ASSISTANT FOOTBALL COACH, UNIVERSITY OF ARKANSAS

"I highly recommend a careful study of this book to any man who truly desires a life of real significance."

WILLIAM K. HALL, PRESIDENT, WILLIAM K. HALL, INC. FINANCIAL STRATEGISTS

"Ronnie Floyd knows what makes and breaks men. This book is a fastball into the strike zone of every man's heart. It clearly defines how to hit a home run in life and eternity, rather than strike out. This is a 'thumbs up' book!"

DR. JIM HENRY, PASTOR, FIRST BAPTIST CHURCH, ORLANDO, FLORIDA

"In a day when the enemy is bombarding society with all his fury and falsehoods, God needs more than a 'few good men.' He needs a host of godly men to seize the hour! The Meaning Of A Man is a training manual for those men who dare to become spiritual champions."

DR. MORRIS H. CHAPMAN, PRESIDENT AND CHIEF EXECUTIVE OFFICER, EXECUTIVE COMMITTEE, SOUTHERN BAPTIST CONVENTION

"Here is a 'must read' for every man who wants to be a real winner. Ronnie Floyd packs a knockout punch with this book, a book that's biblically grounded, powerfully compelling, and intensely practical."

DR. STEVEN J. LAWSON, PASTOR, DAUPHIN WAY BAPTIST CHURCH, MOBILE, ALABAMA

"As biblical as the Word, as relevant as today—that's who Ronnie Floyd is and that's what his book is. Your heart will burn to be a champion for Christ as you live these pages with the author and his Champion."

DR. JOHN R. BISAGNO, PASTOR, FIRST BAPTIST CHURCH, HOUSTON, TEXAS

"Ronnie Floyd has given us a book which is a 'must read' for men. Dr. Floyd's book is strong meat. That's good. Strong meat produces strong men. Read this book and be a stronger man!"

DR. JERRY VINES, FIRST BAPTIST CHURCH, JACKSONVILLE, FLORIDA

"The Meaning Of A Man could not have come at a more opportune time in our nation's history. We are in desperate need of a new breed of men—men who are spiritual champions."

Dr. Thomas D. Elliff, Pastor, First Southern Baptist Church, Del City, Oklahoma

"Ronnie Floyd, who writes with the passion of a pastor and the vision of a leader, sets the issues squarely before Christian men. The Meaning Of A Man sets the record straight, holds the standard high, and points the way to true manhood."

R. Albert Mohler, Jr., President, The Southern Baptist Theological Seminary

"The Meaning Of A Man is exactly the kind of book men are looking for today. Practical, leaving nothing to a guy's imagination, chocked full of masculine illustrations—a man's book. It is honest and hard hitting, but told in unmistakably biblical language that tells men how to be the spiritual champions they yearn to be. I predict this book will achieve success."

Dr. Harold E. O'Chester, Great Hills Baptist Church, Austin, Texas

"Ronnie Floyd knows 'the meaning of a man.' He is running his own race to win, and in his new book, he takes us along with him. Read it and reap!"

Dr. O.S. Hawkins, Pastor, First Baptist Church, Dallas, Texas

"This book is written by a man whom I know to be a spiritual champion in his own right. He gives solid, biblical, practical advice on how every man can be a champion in his home, work place, church, and community. May God use this book to raise up spiritual champions for the Lord Jesus Christ all over our nation."

Dr. James Merritt, Pastor, First Baptist Church, Snellville, Georgia

"If you have a desire to be a champion for Christ and to be your best for Him, that He might be glorified through you, I challenge you to read this book next!"

Dr. Johnny M. Hunt, Pastor, First Baptist Woodstock, Woodstock, Georgia

"If you have wanted to be and worked hard at being a spiritual champion, The Meaning Of A Man will help you find the steps to reach that goal."

Dr. Stephen Arterburn, The Minirth Meier New Life Clinics

"This handbook for men offers a clear, biblically-based, sports-minded approach that can make any man a spiritual champ. Dr. Ronnie Floyd is one of God's choice 'difference makers,' and I'm confident that God will use The Meaning Of A Man as a tool to prepare men for victorious living in the game of life."

T. Ray GrandStaff, Director, Arkansas Fellowship of Christian Athletes

"Dr. Floyd brings you to the bottom line: Men who are partners with Jesus Christ to make a difference."

Dr. Jack B. Johnson, President of the Radio and Television Commission, Southern Baptist Convention

"This is a book for our day."

Dr. Kenneth S. Hemphill, President, Southwestern Baptist Theological Seminary.